about conflict, to focus on the right things, and to realize better outcomes."

Dave Collyer, Corporate Director

"The major contribution [Mark] made is to develop an effective process for transforming a highly complex conflict into inputs that are amenable to the application of the graph model for conflict resolution methodology... Given the importance of making the best choice in 'wicked problem' situations like Northern Gateway, the work completed here can provide a new avenue for gaining insights and making effective decisions. [Mark] builds on, and extends, the time-tested GMCR framework and clearly demonstrates that the model can be applied to one of the most challenging multi-stakeholder environmental issues facing us now."

Dr. Tom Keenan, University of Calgary

"I spend most of my time on the ground on the front lines of a very complicated project, managing lots of interpersonal dynamics and complex people issues. I find Mark's weekly strategy updates to be helpful because I don't have time to dig into all the things he uncovers. It runs the gamut from high-level policy issues down to interpersonal dynamics that the engagement team can chase down or at least be aware of."

Manager, Indigenous Relations

"Our team has found Dr. Szabo's approach to be helpful in navigating complicated land issues. We especially appreciated his concept of Focal Thinking and the idea that complex conflicts should not be approached as negotiations."

Vice President, Land & Stakeholder Engagement

"I have known of, and worked directly with, Dr. Szabo for many years now. He has an uncanny knack for turning complicated ideas, topics, and issues into straightforward strategies for action. He also understands the critical role of persuasive communications in navigating human complexity, and we at Anstice value his collaborative approach and team-oriented way of getting stuff done."

Sheenah Rogers-Pfeiffer, CEO, Anstice

"I always look forward to Mark's weekly updates, because he has a way of putting the entire project in context and put things in a different light. As I try to navigate all the government relationships I appreciate his outside perspective on what is usually a pretty wide range of topics."

Director, Government Affairs

"So much of engagement work is dealing with complex layers of human emotions and values. Mark's unique approach to navigating that complexity really helps us match up the hard project realities with what's important to the folks on the ground. And at head office."

Manager, Stakeholder Engagement

"One of the recurring themes faced by HR executives in the current age is finding senior leaders who not only understand complexity within an organization, but also know how to react when that organization meets external challenges. My wish is that the concept of Focal Thinking enables every leader, regardless of industry, to meet and resolve the complexity of those challenges."

Brendan Rothwell, Senior Business Advisor

"I have watched Mark's progression in this space from the beginning, and I'm very impressed with how he has been able to take a very complicated academic theory and turn it into something incredibly practical and useful. He draws on his background in law, business, and communications to apply his approach to complex conflicts in a very unique and compelling way."

Sr. Business Analyst, Environmental Engineering

"I appreciate the way Mark understands the critical role that boards play in providing strategic direction to large organizations. He understands governance, policy, and the importance of conflict risk mitigation from a board perspective."

Andrea Goertz, Board Member, Boardwalk REIT

"I've had Mark come to speak to a few of my engagement teams, and they always find his unique perspective very useful. He has a way of helping put very complex issues in context, and that context enables folks to build strategies that take into account the complete range of an issue—which of course is mission-critical to any engagement design. He also has a great way of connecting with people and making challenging content accessible and easy to understand. On top of that, he's an incredibly engaging speaker with a lovely sense of humor. I look forward to the next time I'm able to utilize Mark's talent set."

Kevin Thorvaldson, Senior Stakeholder Engagement Leader

"I have had the pleasure of working with Mark since 2010. Mark is off the charts bright, has a laser-sharp and witty communication style, and is gifted at taking apart complex challenges and building understandable strategies. He's a passionate advocate for creating persuasive experiences, and he gets things done!"

Susan Merchant, Facilitator

"Mark is unique in that he is able to take the maelstrom that typically exists within client organizations and is able to turn it into an actionable strategy, all while making the client feel like they were responsible for it all. He can do this because he is able to connect with people and get right to the heart of the matter, regardless of their position on the org chart. I genuinely appreciate Mark's collaborative attitude and willingness to explore new ideas and figure out how we can partner together to resolve a client challenge."

Edgar Baum, CEO at Strata Insights, Post-Graduate Lecturer

Fight Different

The Power of Focal Thinking™
in Systemic Conflicts

Dr. Mark Szabo, Ph.D.

To

Bill, Ruth, Victoria, Dr. Miklós,

Noreen, Dr. Bob,

Dr. Terry, LeAnne, Dr. Michelle,

Dr. Mike, Karen,

and

Vivian, Michael and Jennifer Szabo

Szabo+Partners Ltd.
Calgary, Alberta

ISBN: 978-1-7774235-0-6 (paperback)
ISBN: 978-1-7774235-1-3 (ebook)

www.FocalThinking.com/FightDifferent

CONTENTS

Unless you are going deliberately to prevent a thing being good, you cannot prevent it being worth fighting for.

G. K. Chesterton, *Heretics*

PREFACE

Complicated situations need clarity, but complex ones need *focus*. In a world of systemic conflict, that distinction means everything.

When something is complicated, you can eventually figure out all the moving parts, get clarity on precisely what will happen and know exactly how you should respond. When something is complex, on the other hand, the outcome is unpredictable and its future is both unknown and unknowable.

Clarity doesn't help you when things are unpredictable, because what might be clear right now probably won't stay that way for very long. Clarity is as ephemeral as a paper-thin sheet of ice over a turbulent creek in Springtime.

When a situation is dynamic and unpredictable, we need focus. Focus, unlike clarity, endures in the face of uncertainty. Focus is a movie; clarity is just a picture. Focus is clarity without the expiration date.

The concept of Focal Thinking™ is about how you can bring focus to complexity. It's about training your own mind to be receptive to changing situations and taking action as things change in the moment. More importantly, it's about encouraging, empowering, and persuading others to do the same. The seven principles of Focal Thinking™ are:

1. Don't try to control things that can't be controlled
2. Don't oversimplify things just to feel comfortable
3. Focus on interactions, not outcomes
4. Aim for nudges, not home runs
5. Reintroduce the right kind of complexity back into the system
6. Pay attention to where the actual power lies
7. Prioritize resilience over consistency

Fight Different will show you how to apply these seven principles to complex conflicts so you can help move them from being destructive to constructive human systems.

As human society becomes increasingly complex, we're going to need this now more than ever. And we're going to need you, specifically, to show the right kind of leadership.

INTRODUCTION

Uncertainty is an uncomfortable position.
But certainty is an absurd one.

Voltaire, *Letter to Frederick William II*

C onflict can be the bridge between what is and what should be. Conflict can be where we innovate, create, and design something unique out of something ordinary. Like the incoming and outgoing tides locked in their eternal struggle to sustain life and keep our world from being deluged, conflict can be where we sharpen each other. Push each other. Test each other.

If we get it right.

But if we get it wrong, conflict can turn against us and everyone involved. What can create can also destroy. What can build can also tear down.

Fight Different is about leading strategically in the face of large, chaotic, multiparty conflicts. The really big ones. The ones with dozens and dozens, perhaps hundreds, of conflicting people, groups, organizations, stakeholders, and the public. It's about knowing what to do next, and why to do it, in the middle of very chaotic situations.

I want you to win. I genuinely do. Your ability to grapple with the full range of complexity in a conflict will lead you to better solutions for everyone involved. You're going to help lead humanity to better outcomes, one conflict at a time. You'll need to be aware upfront, however, that this is not for everyone. This may not win you many friends because people tend to be comfortable with how they choose to make sense of the world. It might not make you popular, but it will definitely help you lead in challenging times.

1

My goal here is to encourage and equip like-minded leaders who want to help society engage in big conflicts strategically, respectfully, and effectively. I'm going to show you how to harness the power of complexity science to make sense of complex conflicts, build practical strategies to turn them into creative forces and stay resilient in the face of constant, inexorable change.

My approach, which I call Focal Thinking™, is going to get you ready to handle a whole new level of complexity. Focal Thinking™ is about nuances and nudges and resiliently adapting to chaotic situations. It will enable you to pay attention to just the right things at just the right time and avoid the distracting noise. It'll make complicated situations work for you, not against you. It'll turn chaos into an ally and complexity into a welcome friend. It'll turn enemies into grudgingly respectful antagonists. It's fatal to stereotypes, partisanship, and muddled thinking. If you spend some time with me, you're going to end up with some powerful tools that will empower you to show strategic leadership in complex conflict situations. The seven principles of Focal Thinking™ are:

1. Don't try to control things that can't be controlled
2. Don't oversimplify things just to feel comfortable
3. Focus on interactions, not outcomes
4. Aim for nudges, not home runs
5. Reintroduce the right kind of complexity back into the system
6. Pay attention to where the actual power lies
7. Prioritize resilience over consistency

There are some outstanding books about complex conflict *within* organizations, but precious few about complex conflicts *outside* the organization. When we try to accomplish something big and bring it into the world, things get complex because of the human element. Unlike the physical and technical aspects of large projects, the human landscape is an entirely different environment. It's unknown territory for many people because we are not necessarily trained in dealing with the squishy stuff. The non-technical requirements. The emotions. The (apparent) illogic. It's like we're all speaking a different language. And now more than ever, this gets in the way of how people want to live out their closely-held values. Where a complexity-based approach really shines is when you turn it loose into the wild.

Most leaders are still trained to think linearly, but the world is chaotic. It's been said that nature doesn't build in straight lines, but we tend to think in straight lines. When our lines bump up against nature's curves, we inevitably get a reminder of who's in charge. We often end up ill-equipped for the realities of nature's complexity because we apply linear thinking to a world that won't straighten out for us. The science tells us that we run into trouble when we oversimplify complex situations in our rush to take action. That's why we miss cues and nuances that would otherwise let us move forward and keep the conflict creative.

Fight Different describes how to use Focal Thinking™ and the science behind complex natural systems as applied to human conflict. As it turns out, examining complex conflicts this way provides us with some practical, down-to-earth ways to navigate through them.

If you're ready for an intense journey for yourself and those counting on your strategic leadership, the art and science of Focal Thinking will get you launched in a whole new direction. And as these things tend to do, it will include a bit of self-discovery.

Let's get started.

SECTION ONE: THE NATURE OF THE PROBLEM

I'm grateful you're going to start this book because it means you want to get yourself ready to make a difference. I know you're going to help advance your own work and career, but I also know that if we do this right, you're going to also make your part of the world a better place. I know this because you're going to create the kind of conditions that will help turn destructive conflicts into creative ones. Based on the science related to complex conflicts, that's going to mean creating new interactions between people, breaking down stereotypes, and making sure we and our teams are nimble enough to adjust and pivot on a moment's notice when new opportunities come along to make things better.

We're going to look at complex conflicts from a natural systems perspective, and this first section will look at the root of the problem that causes these types of conflicts. The overall goal is for you to be able to show strategic leadership in a complex conflict, so we'll need to make sure we're clear on what that actually looks like. The objective is going to be to create the right mindset for yourself because it's our own thinking that will either help or hinder our ability to make sense of complex conflicts and be useful to others. The problem we're going to face along the way is something I call the Coherence Trap, and it's what some of the science tells us is the biggest obstacle to dealing with complex conflicts.

Showing Strategic Leadership

My goal is for you to increase your ability to show strategic leadership in complex conflicts. Strategic leadership is a nice pair of buzzwords, so let's start off by making sure we're talking about the same thing.

For the purposes of this book, strategic leadership, when dealing with a complex conflict, is the ability to know exactly what to do next, and why to do it.

That's it.

It sounds simple, but in the context of complex conflicts, that's no small thing. To be able to show up, day after day, and know exactly what to do next, and why to do it, in the face of constant change, frustration, and emotional turmoil. That's going to be quite an accomplishment. And it's well within your grasp.

For those of us who are involved with complex conflicts, either as leaders, advisors, or participants, we have to make sense of complex conflicts in order to do our job. As leaders, one of our primary roles is guiding people through conflict situations. In many ways, we are defined by the problems we solve, and the bigger and more complicated the conflict, the more important we are seen to be. Leaders who solve small matters remain small leaders. Leaders need to make sense of complex conflicts because that is what is expected of us. That's part of what defines the role of a leader in the first place; the ability to lead people out of a situation from which they cannot navigate on their own. Your ability to get people from point A to point B is why they put their trust in you in the first place. If we are not able to make sense of a complex conflict ourselves, we cannot expect to lead anyone through it.

Professionals who advise on conflicts have a similar motivation. If we can't rise above the complexity of a conflict and find a path through it, we add no value for our clients and will soon be looking for other work. For advisors, the issue is slightly different from what it is for leaders, however. They are called upon to help organizations cope with exceptionally complicated conflicts because that is their specialty.

Leaders can fail to bring a team or organization through a conflict and find reasons for their inability to do so and still keep their jobs because they have other roles within the organization. Conflict advisors have nowhere to hide. In many ways, they are only as good as the last conflict they helped navigate, so all eyes are on them.

Participants who find themselves, for whatever reason, in conflicts have different pressures. They may either be actively or passively involved. Those who are actively involved are there because they are the proponent or an opponent of something that creates a conflict; for example, a company proposing a pipeline or activists who oppose it. Participants can also be passively involved if others have imposed something on them. The landowner of a proposed wind farm may not want to be involved, but they have no choice in the matter.

Participants in a conflict can run the gamut of motivations, from those who are just doing their jobs to those who are emotionally invested in the outcome. That said, it is very difficult for participants to stay dispassionate about the conflict and their involvement for very long because complex conflicts end up being complex in the first place because they are about values as much as they are about issues. The more values-heavy the conflict, the more passionate the participants, so for them, the ability to effectively engage in a conflict goes deeper than their professions; it speaks to who they are as individuals. Leaders, advisors, and participants all have different motivations for how to make sense of complex conflicts and their role in them, but the struggles they face have a common element.

I like to think of strategy as being a process that keeps going long after the consultants have been paid, the whiteboards are erased, the reams of paper have been printed, the reports are duly cataloged and stored on a shelf, and senior management congratulates themselves for a job well done. What is left will either provide a clear roadmap of action for everyone else, or a 37-point plan that will gather dust in an obscure storage closet. We need a roadmap of action, but the problem with complex conflicts is that as soon as you print the map, it's out of date. Your solutions need to be resilient enough to live on in the face of constant change, and you, as a strategic leader, are expected to guide the entire process the entire time.

That means as things constantly change, you need to show up with exactly what to do next (so you can guide folks), and whom to do it (so you can get mobilize them into action). No pressure.

Wrap-Up and What's Next

You'll notice I tend to favor action-based definitions. For example, in my view leaders are people who have followers. Nothing more, nothing less. If you don't have people following what you say or do, then you're not actually a leader. Similarly, strategy is only as good as what happens once the wheels have been set in motion. If things only work when you are there to oversee them, you didn't actually have a strategy, you just had a plan. When you combine those two definitions, your ability to provide strategic leadership will prove itself if the people doing what you say have the right impact even when you're not around to watch over things. For them to get to that point, they need to know what to do, when to do it, and why. For that to happen, first you need to know that yourself.

Next, we're going to look one of the most important steps to getting yourself ready for showing strategic leadership in complexity. Spoiler Alert: it happens between your ears.

Getting the Right Mindset

There is only one way to happiness, and that is to cease worrying about things which are beyond the power of our will.

Epictetus, *Discourses, Book 4*

As we'll be discussing throughout this book, the key to successfully showing strategic leadership in complex conflicts involves cultivating the right mindset, not just in others, but more in ourselves. I've got a quick story that really captures the mindset we're aiming for.

I had an experience a few years back that made a big impact on me and, in some ways, led to the book you are reading or listening to right now. I was on business in London with a colleague. This was back in the good old days when you could take liquids and gels onto a plane. My colleague and I were on our way back home, and when we got to the airport, security was a nightmare. That happened to be the day they had decided to change the rules and not allow liquids and gels on planes, and they were just in the process of implementing that new procedure. My colleague had checked his liquids and gels in his luggage, so it wasn't a problem for him, but I had not. This was also before the new terminal in Heathrow, and so it was still a bit of a convoluted system.

My colleague was able to sail through security, but I had to go through what was to be a Kafkaesque nightmare. We had been running a bit late getting to the airport and didn't have the extra cushion of time that I usually like to have, so I was already a little bit tense. When the ticket agent explained the task ahead of me, I felt even worse. She helpfully explained that I needed to go and get my bag from the luggage handling area, but that meant I would then have to go through customs again and then take the Tube to the right terminal. It didn't make much sense to me, and I could feel my blood pressure rising, so I got started making my way to the next roadblock as quickly as possible. I was on a mission.

Once my bags finally came, I had to stand in line for customs to re-enter the country so I could get on the Tube to the next terminal. The customs agent looked at me dubiously and asked, "How long do you intend to stay in the country?" I told her that I was just trying to get to the next terminal, and she gave me a part-condescending, part-pitying look and wished me luck. I finally made it down to the Tube station, and there was a thronging sea of humanity ahead of me. Apparently, this new procedure caused a huge problem, and I was just one of the many.

At this point, I was in full panic mode. I don't do well in large crowds, especially when they are getting in the way of something I need to accomplish. Like getting home. I pushed my way onto the Tube and, of course, it malfunctioned. We were all sitting in the dark for only 10 minutes, but it seemed like an eternity. Once they got running again, I was able to make my way to the stairs towards the terminal. As I started running up the two long flights (the escalators were under repair, naturally), I started to think I might actually make it. It was going to be close, but that hope spurred me on to action. I jumped over suitcases. I weaved between slow-moving people. I was alive. I was exhausted. I was still terrified at the idea of missing my plane, but I had hope. Finally, I could see the ticketing gate. Great news! There was no lineup. That should have tipped me off that something was wrong, but I was blinded by excitement and fear.

I proudly (and redundantly) announced my arrival at the ticketing desk and asked what to do next. The two agents had been in mid-conversation, and I had apparently interrupted them. They stopped talking to each other, and both slowly turned and looked at me with the same sort of look you might give to a small child interrupting an adult conversation. The agent on the left said, "Can we help you?" I said, "Yes! I am on this flight, and I finally ran the gauntlet to get here. What do I need to do next?"

The one agent said, "We can get you your ticket, but you still need to go through security." Then he pointed to the security line. As I slowly turned to look, my heart sank. All the people who were missing from the ticketing area were jammed into an enormous hallway, with people as far as the eye could see. It was like being at the back of a concert venue. I went completely numb. There was no way I was going to get home. I froze. To his credit, the agent did his best to hide his amusement. He could see that I needed some measure of consolation, and I'll never forget what he said to me.

"Mate, sometimes it's better when you just give up hope."

That hit me like a bolt of lightning. He was right. Infuriating, but absolutely right. And once it sunk in that there was absolutely no way I was getting on the plane, despite all of my efforts and all of my striving, I suddenly felt a unique sense of peace. As the alternative was taken away from me, I felt a sense of lightness, like I was floating above this whole unfortunate experience.

I felt free and light as soon as I submitted to the reality of my situation. Once it was out of my control, I could just relax a little bit and find a way to make the most of the situation. I thought to myself, Well then, I will just have to have an adventure, won't I? Then the agent also wisely said, "Why don't you get yourself a nice hotel, enjoy your evening, and come back in the morning, and we'll get you home." I thanked the agents for the valuable life lesson and said I would see them tomorrow—nice and early.

Hope can be a destructive force when it is based on faulty or incomplete information. Had I known what I was really in for, I would have never hoped to make my flight. I would have just relaxed, found a hotel, and enjoyed another day in London. I would have saved myself all the anxiety and fear. Giving up when there is no hope is sometimes the best course of action. We do not have to give up hope entirely; we just need to place it somewhere else.

What I discovered from this experience is that if you can get yourself to the point where you can release yourself from the need to control the situation, observe things as they are from a wider perspective, and then revisit what you want to try and do, you can accomplish pretty much anything. Let's call that "ROR" for short: Release. Observe. Revisit.

In his book, *Stillness is the Key*, Ryan Holiday describes the process used by archery master Awa Kenzo to achieve the kind of inner stillness needed to block distractions and focus one's creative energy.

"What we need in life... is to loosen up, to become flexible, to get to a place where there is nothing in our way—including our own obsession with certain outcomes… Mastering our mental domain—as paradoxical as it might seem—requires us to step back from the rigidity of the word 'mastery.' We'll get the stillness we need if we focus on the individual steps, if we embrace the process, and give up *chasing*… The closer we get to mastery, the less we care about specific results. The more collaborative and creative we are able to be, the less we will tolerate ego or insecurity. The more at peace we are, the more productive we can be." [1]

The reason I mention it now is because if we can get to that sort of mindset, then we'll be able to navigate anything complex. In fact, what I discovered in my research and over the years in practice is that if you can't get to that mindset of ROR, you'll never be able to navigate anything complex, let alone a complex conflict.

Wrap-Up and What's Next

It's all well and good to be Zen and chill about complex issues, but we all know that's easier said than done. It's great for some master archer to talk about stillness and trusting the process, but all he needs to do is teach people how to hit a target with an arrow. He's not dealing with shareholders, board members, executives, protesters, clients, and any number of people trying to get what they all need from you.

Fair enough.

And yet, the fact remains that unless you can find your way to that state of ROR, stillness, Zen or whatever you want to call it, you're not going to be able to show up with strategic leadership in the midst of a complex conflict. The rest of this book will show you why that's true, why it's so important and how to get to the point where you can ROR in any complex conflict you might be facing. Once we get ourselves to that state of mind, anything is possible.

Next, we're going to look at the single most important reason conflicts start, metastasize, and elude resolution: The Coherence Trap.

Overcoming The Coherence Trap

The big challenge that we face when dealing with complex conflicts starts with us. The hard truth is that it's our own way of thinking that starts them and prevents them from being constructive. You may say that you're just trying to get a project to move forward, not create conflict. And that, right there, is a perfect example of what we're talking about. Even if we have the best intentions, we don't always make things better.

Here's what happens. As we bump up against something we don't fully understand, our brains push us to make sense of it. This happens whether we have all the information available or not, or whether all the information is even possible to have or not. Psychologists call that the need for *coherence*. It's part of how our minds evolved to keep us safe. In a complex conflict, the evolutionary drive to make sense of things above all else means that we force ourselves to come to conclusions about it that may not square with reality. That causes us to miss the nuances and subtleties that might point the way to solving the thing.

I call this the *Coherence Trap* because that overriding need we have for coherence can trap us into ways of thinking that make complex conflicts endure and avoid becoming constructive.

During my little adventure at Heathrow airport, my emotions clouded my thinking about the situation in a way that made it infinitely more challenging than necessary. It was based on faulty information that lead to a kind of false hope that made things worse for me. A complex conflict acts the same way.

The biggest challenge we face when trying to make sense of conflicts is our own way of thinking. If we think linearly and logically about a complex, emotional conflict, we're never going to fully grasp what's actually going on. At some point, that complexity becomes too much to wrap our minds around, and we start grasping for anything that will help us make sense of it. In other words, the same kind of thinking that prevents us from understanding conflicts is the same thinking that got us there in the first place. That is part of what makes them so difficult.

In the section after this, we're going to talk about why our normal approach to thinking about conflicts doesn't scale up to meet the challenge, but first, we need to talk about what goes on in our own minds. Our response is critical, and if we're going to be more effective, we'll need to understand what's creating that response in the first place. We're going to have to think about our own process of thinking, so hang on while we poke around in your brain a little bit.

As we mentioned, our need for coherence is a concept from psychology that says we will do pretty much anything to make sure our understanding of reality lines up with what we observe. In the face of complexity and uncertainty, we feel a fundamental drive to reduce tension, disorientation, and dissonance.[2] And here's the kicker; we will even prioritize our need for coherence above having all the facts. We need things to make sense. We need to make sure what we believe aligns with what we see. It is a perfectly natural and appropriate response to how we function in the world, and it's part of our evolutionary ability to keep ourselves alive.

The problem comes when our urge to create coherence ignores the fact that we don't have all the facts. The lack of information, for example, that usually comes with a complex conflict. When we try to align our thinking and feeling with reality, but we can't actually see all of reality, we fall into the Coherence Trap. This is what happens when we feel the need to be right, rather than accurate.[3] Situations like conflicts, which are values-laden and emotional in nature, often spur us into action on short notice. The adrenaline kicks in, and the powerful emotions push us to act. When a thing is complex, our urge to act may quickly overtake our ability to get all the information we might need. To do this we take shortcuts, and that's where we get ourselves into trouble. That is what helps create complex conflicts and keep them alive for a long time.[4]

Here's an example. Many will resort to stereotypes of those on the other side of a conflict as a way to make sense of the values and issues and chaos. Stereotypes are basically just a convenient oversimplification. A helpful shorthand to get you started. However, people who stereotype each other are not very likely to engage authentically. Complex conflicts can even push this to extremes, to the point that participant's urge for coherence overshadows what is in their own interest. Self-interest is a hallmark of normal, healthy rationality, but it is often missing in conflicts, particularly those that endure to the detriment of all involved.[5] How many times have you seen people act to their own detriment, just to prove a point? Now expand that by hundreds of people.

If we're going to avoid the Coherence Trap, it will help if we understand its stages so we can keep an eye out and be aware of our own reactions.

Stage One: Confusion

Our first natural response to overwhelming complexity is confusion. When you feel this, that's your first warning sign that the Coherence Trap may be just ahead. Beware! In my consulting practice helping companies with complex conflicts, this is a regular occurrence. We'll talk about this later in the book, but one of the first things I recommend is doing a human landscape model of a conflict, so you have a definitive, comprehensive map of all the participants and organizations involved. This can be incredibly confusing, especially at the early stages, because there is simply too much to know or assimilate all at once. It's just not possible. If you're going to be involved in complex conflicts, you're going to need to accept the fact that confusion will be your constant companion. And you'll need to get comfortable with it because once it's gone, you can guarantee it'll be coming back very soon. The goal will be to put that confusion in a small little box somewhere it can't cause you any trouble. In the meantime, that feeling of confusion is something you'll need to watch out for and be mindful of. Once you get good at the art and science of Focal Thinking, you'll get to the point where you welcome that feeling of confusion because you know you'll soon have a breakthrough, the clouds will part, the sun will shine on you, and you'll be able to tell folks what to do next, and why to do it. You'll know that state of ROR is just around the corner.

Stage Two: Discomfort

When we're confused about what's going on, our first natural go-to emotion is discomfort, but only if we care about the situation. If it's something we're not invested in or close to, it's easy to shrug off confusion because it has no real cost. However, if you play a role in a conflict—as a leader, advisor, or participant—confusion has a huge cost because it gets in the way of what you need to accomplish. If you are supposed to be leading people from point A to point B in a conflict, and you have no idea what's actually going on, this puts your livelihood at risk. The same can be said for a consulting advisor; you're not much good to anyone if you're as confused as everyone else. For participants on the job or as a "civilian," it's also very uncomfortable because your values or property may be at risk.

If you're part of the conflict and you care about what happens, confusion is going to lead to discomfort. This is where that evolutionary urge for coherence kicks in, and you'll have that overwhelming need to make sense of the confusion at all costs. You'll need to treat this as a warning sign, too, just like you'll do with confusion. I get this all the time when I'm confused about all the moving parts of a conflict because, for me, it's critical that I get a handle on things. But it never fails. As soon as I start building a strategy or revise a strategy based on new information (something you'll be doing constantly), that sense of panic kicks in because I have absolutely no idea where it's going to lead or how I'm going to make sense of it all. Confusion is one thing, but discomfort takes it to a new level. As before, the goal here is going to be to help you keep a lid on the discomfort and trust the process that's going to help you get it all under control. In the meantime, keep an eye on yourself and make sure you're not giving in to the panic.

Stage Three: Oversimplification

If you do it wrong, you will want to start grasping at any scrap of anything that you can understand to get rid of that confusion. Like a drowning man grabbing for anything that floats, confusion and discomfort usually make us reach for the nearest flotsam and jetsam to keep our head above water. As we discussed earlier, that piece of driftwood we just grabbed might have been nearby, but it's also just one of the hundreds floating nearby. The reality of the situation may be a lot more nuanced than we know, yet we still need to grab on to something. Oversimplification comes in many guises. Stereotypes are a big one you often see in complex conflicts. One group stereotypes the other as a way to feel good about themselves and make the others' unfathomable differences appear understandable. So-and-so is against pipelines because they hate capitalism. That guy hates the environment because he's a tool of the corporate greed machine.

And on it goes.

Using a pipeline project example, imagine two friends having a coffee together, chatting about the relative merits of a pipeline to transport liquid natural gas versus using a train. They might discuss the impact of diesel emissions as compared to zero emissions from a pipeline. They might debate the danger of a train derailment versus a pipeline leak in which the LNG would simply dissipate into the atmosphere. They might contrast the impact of a greenfield linear pipeline on the landscape versus that of an existing line of a railway. It would be an enjoyable, robust, and informative discussion. They might agree on the outcome, and they might not. Even if they didn't agree on everything, the interaction would be valuable and enhance their ongoing relationship. Who knows? They might even create an entirely new way of accomplishing things. Admit it; you'd like to be part of that discussion.

Now imagine these two people differently. One of them is wearing a business outfit, and she wears the pinky ring of a professional engineer (that's a Canadian thing). The other is wearing combat fatigues with an anarchy patch, and his ring happens to be in his nose. Suddenly we might expect to see a very different pattern of interaction—if we can imagine them even agreeing to sit down for a coffee in the first place. We would expect to see very little meaningful exchange of information. We might expect to see defensive behavior, finger-pointing, and personal, ad hominem attacks in the guise of reasoned debate. Neither side would be listening to each other, and very little authentic engagement would likely happen. Now imagine these two people's interaction magnified over hundreds or thousands of people. The results would be precisely what we see in a typical pipeline conflict, where those patterns of interaction create a complex conflict.

When we oversimplify things, we get back our sense of comfort because then we at least have the feeling that we understand what's going on and why people do what they do—especially people we don't agree with. Later we'll go into more depth on the lengths we go to justify our oversimplifications. Some of them are actually downright respectable. They're not always about stereotypes or personal bigotry, even though the result is pretty much the same. For now, the point is simply that we will need to keep watch on our own urge to simplify matters, and never settle in our quest for more knowledge about a situation. In a world where the phrase "the science is settled" is proudly touted by mature adults who should know better, we have to remember that science never actually settles. And neither do Focal Thinkers. Stay, thirsty, my friends. And always keep your eyes open.

Stage Four: Blinders

For those who do unfortunately choose to settle in their thinking, the unfortunate result is blinders. If you purposefully restrict your own thinking just so you can avoid the discomfort of confusion, you're going to be making decisions based on incomplete information. In a complex and fluid conflict, that's going to enable you to make the conflict worse (which may be what you want) or keep the thing going, but it's not going to help you change anything. Choosing this path means you can no longer see all of the nuances and details that are causing that discomfort in the first place. It's a false hope, like me running like an idiot through Heathrow airport, thinking that I was actually going to make it to that plane. Blinders can be a great way to feel better in the short term, but they don't help when it comes to effectively navigating a complex conflict.

Stage Five: Dried-up Patterns of Interaction

Now we come to the crux of the issue. While you and I are fitting ourselves with comfortable blinders and oversimplifying things so that we can avoid a bit of discomfort, guess what? So is everybody else. As we all wander around with our self-imposed blinders on, it's no wonder we're constantly bumping into each other. Later in the book, we'll talk about the fact that complex conflicts behave remarkably like other natural systems, like flocks of birds or schools of fish. Those systems work well because each of the animals knows the rules and focuses on the actions of those nearby. If those interactions were to get scrambled, the whole thing would collapse on itself, just like we see in complex conflicts. It's those patterns of interaction that hold the key. If you change those patterns, you change the entire system. One tweak to the rules of how they interact will send the whole thing in a totally different direction.

The same thing happens when we put on our blinders. We take an otherwise healthy system with functioning patterns of interaction and turn it into a train wreck. When we stop authentically engaging with the "other side," we bring the whole thing to a grinding halt. Those previously healthy patterns of interaction dry up, and we're left with a dying system.

When I was a kid, my parents would scrimp and save to take the family to a tropical island paradise every few years. The place we always stayed had a beautiful coral reef that was teeming with iridescent colors and vibrant life. It was as breathtaking as it was overwhelming. Then one year, we returned, and the whole thing was dead. It looked like a black and white photo of a World War I battlefield. We were told it was part of the natural cycle of the reef, but it was still sad to see the difference. Granted, the living version was the actual battleground where the sea creatures all vied for survival, but it worked. There was a balance to it. The World War I version looked like a battlefield, but it was the opposite. There was no struggle. No engagement. No back-and-forth. Because everything was dead or gone. Sometimes beauty comes from healthy conflict, not the absence of it.

Wrap-Up and What's Next

The rest of the book will look at how to avoid the Coherence Trap in ourselves and in others because that's the starting point for avoiding destructive conflict and for reinvigorating a dead zone. As we do this, keep in mind that you'll want to start getting in the habit of watching your own reactions and managing your own energy around any conflict you're facing. The simple act of paying attention to our own reactions helps remove us from the urgency and emotions of a situation because it reminds us that there is a pattern and rhythm to these things, and we can react in any way we choose to. One of my favorite philosophers, Epictetus, wrote, "It's not what happens to you, but how you react to it that matters," and "We are disturbed not by things, but by the view which we take of them."

Back to my Heathrow adventure. There was a great deal of uncertainty as to whether I was going to make it through the gauntlet of bureaucracy and humanity, and that uncertainty caused me confusion and discomfort. So I chose to oversimplify the situation and be solely focused on getting to the ticket agent. That makes all the sense in the world, but it caused me to miss a few important details along the way, not the least of which is the fact that there was no possible way I was ever going to get on that plane. That would've been an important detail. So the blinders that I put on myself caused me to miss that vital fact and heightened my stress levels beyond what they should have been. Once I was able to release myself from the need to have control over that situation and step back and observe the reality of it, and I was able to revisit my approach and realize that I could have a perfectly enjoyable and productive experience if I just gave up and got a hotel for the night. That need to make sense of, and have coherence about, a situation steeped in uncertainty caused me no end of grief. It probably also frustrated more than a few people around me who I may or may not have bumped into along the way.

When you find yourself feeling confused about a complex conflict, don't feel uncomfortable; remind yourself that's just the first stage of the Coherence Trap talking to you. If you do find yourself getting uncomfortable about it, try to avoid jumping to conclusions and oversimplifying matters. It's not worth feeling better to purposefully make yourself ignorant. That may be bliss for some people, but you have a job to do, and your bliss will come from success. If you do notice that you've slipped your blinders on and you're making it difficult to authentically engage, take them off and start from the beginning. Focal Thinkers do not settle for anything less than transparency when dealing with others. Now that you know how this works, you're never going to look at conflicts the same way again. And we're just getting started.

Next, we will have a look at the nature of complex conflicts and go deeper into why they are different from negotiations.

SECTION TWO: THE NATURE OF CONFLICTS

Now we're going to spend some time talking about the nature of complex conflicts. If we take some time to examine what creates them and makes them tick, we're going to be much more effective at getting ourselves to a mental state where we can think about them in a focused manner. As Master Kenzo will break down archery into component processes, we're going to pick apart complex conflicts so we can really get a sense of what's going on under the surface.

This section will start off with some important definitions so we can be clear on important terminology and nuances of meaning. We will then go deep on the critical differences between conflicts and negotiations, covering why they require very different treatment. We will finish the section with a discussion of one of our most important coping mechanisms for dealing with complexity and how it actually can make things worse for us and everyone involved.

Defining Conflict

The first thing we will need to get clear on is how we're going to define conflict. For our purposes, I like the definition used by the same people whose scientific theory I found most helpful in developing this approach in the first place. Social psychologists examine group behavior from the perspective of individuals. Sociologists study group behavior as well, but they don't necessarily prioritize the role of how people think and feel. Given that complex conflicts often revolve around a few key individuals—even the very large ones—I found that perspective offers a few more essential tools.

Vallacher et al. suggest this definition of conflict (emphasis mine):

"We define conflict as *a relational process that is influenced by the perception of incompatible activities...* These processes typically occur in a relational context that provides a sense of history and a normative trajectory. In other words, the perception of incompatible activities can function to redefine the manner in which the parties to a relationship think about and act toward one another."[6]

In other words, conflict is when people think others are blocking them, and it changes how they interact over time. For our purposes, we'll just stick with *"relationships influenced by the perception of incompatible activities."* Let's take a moment to unpack that.

First, the idea that relationships in a conflict can be *fluid* helps explain what we see in complex conflicts, especially when participants change their perceptions of each other and of the conflict over time. If that weren't the case, we might as well give up, go home, and stop trying to resolve anything. Second, the focus on *perception* helps explain how and why two or more parties can look at the same set of facts and draw divergent conclusions. It doesn't matter one bit if the activities are actually incompatible; the point is that people think they are. We see this quite often, where two people can argue heatedly about something, only to discover they've been saying the same thing the whole time. Third, *time* is an essential element of any conflict, since they're not necessarily one-off events but more a long series of events strung together. That's definitely true of complex conflicts. Time is also critical because it helps us remember that just because a conflict is in a certain state today, it may all change tomorrow. In fact, it probably will. No, it *definitely* will.

Not everyone agrees with this definition. There is a stream of thought in management literature that looks at conflict as natural pattern fluctuations in a complex organizational system. Andrade, Plowman, & Duchon argue that that organizational conflict is the source of innovation and growth, and rather than being avoided, it should be encouraged:

> "From a complexity view,… conflict can be seen not as noise or error, but rather the fuel that drives system growth and enables learning and adaptive behaviors, which make innovation possible. From a complexity view, the reduction or elimination of conflict is a fool's errand because it requires diminishing the life force of the system itself."[7]

The reason this definition of conflict is not helpful for our purposes is that we're not talking about conflict within an organization; we're talking about what happens out in the wild. Within the confines of an organization, conflict can and should absolutely be harnessed for growth and innovation, and treating large organizations like complex systems offers an important set of managerial tools for leaders of all levels. However, we're talking about external conflicts that happen outside the four walls of an organization; when people aren't having professional disagreements, they want to destroy what you're trying to accomplish.

When it comes to implementing internal innovations and leading organizational growth, defining conflict as inevitable organizational pattern fluctuations is highly recommended and will bear much fruit for any leader. We're just talking about a different context.

As a final thought, you will notice that I prefer to call the people involved in a conflict "participants." It's a neutral term that covers a wide range of levels in which a person can be engaged, and it holds the potential seed of a creative outcome. When you refer to people in conflict as opponents, you've already presupposed a destructive outcome, and in some senses, it's you trying to assert some control over something that's beyond your control. A conflict does not have to include enemies. With conflict "participants," they can go either direction, so it's a helpful term.

There are a few other ideas we should cover at this point because not all conflicts are the same, and we're also not going to be talking about all types of conflicts in this book.

Constructive vs. Destructive Conflict

Not all conflict is bad. Remember my example of the coral reef: when it was teeming with vibrant life, it was full of conflicting animals trying to survive, and when it was dead, there was no conflict at all. As we alluded to in the previous chapter, there is an important stream of thought that says conflict is a necessary part of human interaction. That's how we sharpen and test each other and create new things. The issue for many conflicts is whether they constructively lead towards a better, more authentic understanding between people, or whether they destroy those relationships. For guidance on this, we will return to Vallacher et al., who think of conflicts as existing on a continuum between being constructive and destructive:

"Conflict is far more than a problematic and unwanted feature of human experience. Quite the contrary, conflict is not only a frequent feature of social life, but it is also essential to our survival and progress as a species. Conflict, whether between individuals, groups, or cultures, is necessary for the construction of shared realities, technological and intellectual innovation, and adaptation to novel events and uncertain circumstances. Conflict is inherent in virtually every aspect of human encounter... Conflict per se, then, is neither an exception nor a problem. Constructive conflicts are defined as those which result in mutually satisfactory experiences of the processes, relationships, and outcomes associated with the conflict for all involved parties (Deutsch, 1973). [8] Destructive conflicts are the opposite; in them, at least one of the parties involved experiences dissatisfaction with the conflict."[9]

That's a great way to put it: constructive conflicts allow healthy engagement, and destructive conflicts prevent it. You can even think of difficult and long-lasting conflicts as "a pattern of stable, destructive relations."[10] In a creative conflict, the parties are usually able to adapt to whatever is bringing them into conflict. Not so within a destructive conflict.

I think of this like the tide line, where the outgoing tide bumps up against the incoming tide. If you've ever been on a boat going over a tide line, you'll know that it can get pretty choppy. As the tides collide, they don't give up easily. The outgoing tide desperately wants to get to the open ocean, and the incoming tide needs to get to land. The gravitational force of the moon decides who wins, but the battle still rages. That's a great example of constructive conflict because the outcome is positive for the entire planet, and even though the battle is very real, both sides keep coming back to do their power dance together. If one of them didn't show up, dry land would cease to exist on the planet every 12 hours or so.

Conflict Resolution

Resolution—like beauty, justice, and love—is in the eye of the beholder. One party may consider a conflict resolved if it remains intractable and destructive and never goes away. As we get further into the concepts underlying Focal Thinking, we'll realize that the idea of resolution is as fluid as the conflict itself. An environmental group might disrupt a regulatory engagement process because they'll consider the conflict resolved if it never actually goes away and the project stalls. On the other hand, resolution might mean moving a destructive conflict into the state of being a constructive one where everybody can lose just enough to move things forward. In either case, it hinges on the perception of the observer. To avoid chasing our own tails too much, let's just stick to the idea that resolution means moving a conflict along the continuum to becoming less destructive and more constructive, regardless of the preferred outcome a participant subjectively prefers. And again, don't forget that the conflict is the perception of incompatible activities, so all this is going on inside the minds of the participants.

We're going to go more in-depth on this in the next section, where we're going to compare resolution in a complex conflict context versus a negotiation context. For now, just be prepared to think a bit differently about what resolution means for our purposes.

Complicated vs. Complex

Since we're talking about *complex* conflicts, we should be clear about what that term means. I think you'll find it helpful to our understanding of the nature of complex conflicts if we explain "complex" by contrasting it with its cousin, "complicated." The difference between something complicated and something complex revolves around how much *uncertainty* is involved. Complex things are uncertain; complicated things are not.

Here are a few examples. Think about a watch. I don't mean an electronic watch; I mean a complicated mechanical Swiss watch. Those watches have a very complicated movement inside that is very difficult to figure out. There are a lot of moving parts, and you essentially need a degree in nuclear physics to figure the thing out. But once you do, then you know exactly how it works. And it works the same way, every time. A watch movement is the very definition of certainty. Once it's set in motion, you know exactly what will happen and when it will happen, literally to the very second.

On the other hand, something that is complex is uncertain. Think about our large flock of starlings flying in their undulating, moving mass in the air, which, by the way, is known as a *murmuration*. If you haven't seen this, take a moment to search for "murmuration of starlings." In a murmuration, thousands of birds behaving very much like a school of fish in the ocean as they hunt for food and protect themselves from predators. The murmuration moves and weaves and changes shape constantly and seems to take on a life of its own. There is no leader. No King of the Birds is directing the flock. Each individual bird is focused on the birds in its immediate vicinity. When geese, for example, fly in a "V" formation, they are following the lead bird in an orderly, precise pattern. Not so with a murmuration of starlings. It looks like chaos because that is exactly what it is. Nobody knows where the flock will go or what shape it will take from moment to moment. That is not only unknown; it's *unknowable*. There are a lot of moving parts, and it is definitely complicated, but there is absolutely no way to tell where it's going to go or what it's going to do. It will go anywhere it wants to go, and none of the forethought, observation, or computer modeling in the world is going to help you figure out where that flock will go. That is the very definition of complexity. That unpredictability is what makes a murmuration complex.

When we apply this to conflicts, the differences between complicated and complex become even clearer. A complicated conflict may have many moving parts, but the outcome will be predictable. A good example might be a game of football. The players interact based on clearly defined rules, they are in direct opposition, and even though we do not know which team will win, we can be certain that one team will win. Or perhaps there might be a tie. The game looks complicated, but the outcome is predictable. On the other hand, a "complex" football game would be entirely different. In that case, the players might start the game as usual, but then the fans might rush onto the field, a referee might tear the ball open and put it on his head. The crowd might hoist him on their shoulders, and they'd all march out of the stadium to slather the surrounding city with pudding. Nobody would have predicted that. I would, however, pay double my cable bill to see that on ESPN.

A better example of a complex conflict might be a pipeline routing dispute like the Northern Gateway project in western Canada. In that conflict, the proponent wanted to build a greenfield (i.e. over virgin land) pipeline from the prairies, over the Rocky Mountains, across many rivers, lakes, and streams, through a few dozen Indigenous territories, eventually ending up at the head of a narrow channel that led to the Pacific Ocean. What could possibly go wrong? That conflict was certainly complicated because of all the many factors involved. But it was also complex because the outcome was impossible to predict. The outcome of the project was not binary, like a football game. There were so many layers of approval and off-ramps for the project; a definitive yes or no was not a likely outcome. But the complexity was not just the multiple outcomes of the project itself, but also in the very changeable perspectives and positions of the conflict participants, which were in a constant state of flux. For our purposes, most conflicts are complicated, but where the outcome is not predictable, the conflict is also complex. And that's what we're focusing on.

Wrap-Up and What's Next

Hopefully, now we'll have a consistent understanding of these essential terms and concepts. I never like to leave that to chance, especially when dealing with ideas that are in common use but may carry additional nuances in our particular context. This is important because it will point to some very helpful science-based tools that will help us overcome the Coherence Trap, get to a state of Heathrow-esque ROR, and ultimately equip ourselves with the ability to show strategic leadership in the face of complex conflicts.

Conflicts are Not Negotiations

One helpful way to understand something is to compare it to something it's not. In our case, I think you'll find it helpful to distinguish conflicts from negotiations. They are not the same thing. Negotiations tend to be complicated, and conflicts lean towards being complex. That complexity comes from a combination of the number of participants involved and the level of emotional, value-heavy decision making. Adding the "human factor" to a larger pool of participants creates an uncertain, dynamic, complex environment.

There are obvious similarities between negotiations and conflicts, but the core differences are so fundamental that it's very dangerous to treat them alike. When we treat one as if it's like the other, we're going to miss those fundamental differences, and that's going to trip us up along the way. It's like getting an invitation to a formal black-tie event but showing up in a rubber chicken suit. If they even let you in the door, you're not going to get the response you were hoping for, and your evening will go quite differently than you might have expected. (Just trust me on this.) If we take a bit of time to think about why that's the case, it will help us lay the groundwork for how we want to show up to a complex conflict in the right way.

In negotiations, we are trying to align interests, but in a conflict, we are struggling with a perception of incompatible activity. That alone should tell us that treating one like the other is not a great idea. Thinking back to the football game analogy, a normal game that follows the rules is more like a negotiation in the sense that the outcome is very certain. Someone is going to win, and someone is going to lose, or maybe there's going to be a tie. That's it. In a negotiation, the parties are either going to come to an agreement, or they're not. You can't tell in advance which of those two things will happen, but one of them will. A conflict is more like that dystopian version of the game where the ref puts the ball on his head, and the crowd puddings the surrounding town. There is any number of possibilities that could happen, and because of the uncertain nature of the conflict, it acts more like that complex system of the flock of birds than a complicated watch movement. Of course, any human endeavor is going to be messy and uncertain on some level. But the difference is that this uncertainty is a defining feature of conflicts, whereas it is merely one element of some negotiations. A conflict centers around uncertainty, whereas a negotiation may simply have some uncertainty associated with it.

With that in mind, let's go a bit deeper into the differences between negotiations and conflicts and see if we can get some more clarity on it all.

Different Sizes

One difference between negotiations and the kind of conflicts we're talking about is the number of participants. In a negotiation, we are trying to align mutual interests, so there is a natural ceiling to the number of participants you can hope to align. The more you add, the harder it is to find space for alignment. Not so with a conflict. In a conflict, there is no natural ceiling to the number of participants because there is no end to the number of people and organizations that could potentially perceive incompatible activities.

In negotiations, there is also usually a higher threshold for joining the proceedings. The price of entry is that you have to have something of specific value to the rest of the participants. If I showed up to a high-stakes game of *chemin de fer* in Monaco, I can guarantee I wouldn't get past the velvet rope or be allowed to even watch the game from a distance. (Particularly if I were wearing that rubber chicken suit. But I digress.) I just don't have anything to offer the other participants. However, the barrier to entry into a conflict is basically nothing. That's even more the case now that anyone can bang out 140 characters into their social media account, jump on their bully pulpit, and join in the fun.

Most negotiations that we'll be involved in are also going to take place within a relatively specific socio-economic group of individuals and organizations, so the pool of potential participants is naturally smaller. Again, not so with conflicts. Anybody and anyone can participate, so the pool is much larger.

As we'll talk about now, the combination of more participants and less "rational" decision-making is a big part of what makes negotiations fundamentally different than conflicts, and it's that "non-rational" decision-making that creates the uncertainty of outcome that drives them into the realm of complexity.

Rational vs. Emotional

An important difference between negotiations and conflicts is that one is more rational, and the other is more emotional. Negotiations are meant to be the rational alignments of mutual interests to the benefit of both parties. If you don't get that alignment, then everybody walks away and looks for other opportunities. A complex conflict is more rooted in emotions. If a conflict is not resolved, it's not like the participants call it a day and walk away from the conflict. Quite the opposite. They're going to keep at it.

Conflicts are about something beyond that pure rationality. It's true that none of us can make a decision without access to our emotions and our rational thinking, so everything we do has an aspect of both. However, conflicts are much more rooted in emotion, and that is absolutely critical to keep in mind when we are looking at ways to navigate our way through it. Part of what makes complex conflicts complex in the first place is the central role that emotion plays. That dramatically increases the level of unpredictability, and it's a big part of why we end up there in the first place.

That's why assuming rational behavior and making rational arguments in the midst of a complex conflict will pretty much ensure we won't find a way through it and will probably only make it worse. For example, when energy companies do nothing but shout facts and statistics and economics at folks trying to protect the environment, that not only fails to solve the conflict, it makes it worse. That's like bringing a knife to a gunfight because the conflict is not just about facts or rationality; it's about emotion and values. Shouting facts just reinforces what the other side already believes about you.

Factoring in the emotional aspects of complex conflicts to the analysis takes us into new territory that many of us are not well-equipped to handle because we're just not trained to think that way. Lacking the tools to account for non-rational behavior not only gets in the way of our ability to make sense of conflicts, but it is also an important part of why complex conflicts perpetuate themselves. When conflict participants find it hard to make sense of complexity, they oversimplify matters and create false internal narratives based on incomplete information. As we discussed, that oversimplification gets in the way of authentic engagement, we land squarely in the Coherence Trap, and the conflict digs in even further. Obviously, there are emotions in a negotiation, but the difference is that negotiations can ignore the emotional component and still succeed.

Let's go a bit deeper into the role of emotions because it's fundamental to understanding this whole process.

One of the most important drivers of uncertainty in conflicts is non-rational behavior. When we say "non-rational," that doesn't mean "irrational" or "crazy." It just means we're acknowledging the fact that sometimes behavior is driven more by rationality and sometimes more by emotion. Both are perfectly logical and normal; one is just more calculated than the other. In reality, it's always a bit of both, because we all make decisions based on emotion and reason. They are the twin wings on which our behavior takes flight. So for our purposes, it's really just a matter of degree.

When we think about why negotiations are complicated, and conflicts are complex, part of what drives that is the unpredictability that comes with non-rational behavior. The scientific literature tells us that emotion-heavy, values-laden decision-making helps turn conflicts into unpredictable, complex systems. Where we have emotion, we have complexity; and emotion, values, and other behavioral drivers are defining characteristics of a complex conflict. In the next section, we will look at the science that helps us know how to work with a complex system, but for now, we just need to know that complexity is driven, in part, by non-rational thinking.

Not surprisingly, applying our negotiation training to complex conflicts doesn't really work. Negotiation techniques usually teach us to separate the people from the problem and the emotions from the issues. In conflicts, the people *are* the problem, and the emotions *are* the issues. That's why treating a conflict like a negotiation is destined to fail, and possibly make it worse. I would argue that the failure to account for the emotions inherent in complex conflicts is one of the most critical shortcomings of our modern age. By treating conflicts as if they are mostly rational negotiations, we miss crucial drivers of the conflict. And we do it on purpose. Repeatedly. Especially if we work for (for example) large, engineering-based companies full of competent, rational people who have been trained to leverage those abilities to maximum effect. You can't feel your way to building a bridge or office tower, and thank goodness people don't try to do that. However, skills in those areas are very different from the ability to navigate an emotion-heavy human landscape.

We'll go more in-depth on the science later in the book, but one additional idea is worth noting at this point: the concept of "self-organization." This is the idea that as system-wide behavior emerges over time, it does so in a way that is not necessarily intended by the participants. In other words, the system seems to take on a life of its own. Complex conflicts resist purely rational decision making because of, according to Vallacher, et al., "the inevitable and spontaneous organization of discrete elements into global patterns that, once formed, resist disruption and other sources of change."[11] Similarly, Merçay & Borrie explain it this way:

"The detailed behavior of a complex adaptive system is fundamentally unpredictable. It is not a question of better understandings of the agents, better models, or faster computing; you simply cannot reliably predict the detailed behavior... through analysis. You have to let the system run to see what happens."[12]

These things happen not as the result of explicit choices by isolated individuals but rather as the result of repeated interactions between multiple individuals over time. In fact, in many cases, the overall collective outcome is vastly different from what any party wanted or intended. Smith & Conrey argue:

"This paradox can occur in an escalating interpersonal or intergroup conflict, where each party is confident that its own incremental escalation will cause the other to back down and give up, but the dynamics of the situation means that conflict instead spirals to an extreme."[13]

How many times have you seen in a conflict where people say, "We never intended it for it to go this far, but it just took on a life of its own." You see this quite often in complex conflicts, where participants get swept up in the group dynamic and do things they hadn't planned on or expected to do. Think back to our murmuration of starlings and how it seems to act as a living, breathing organism in its own right, independent of any leadership from any of the individual birds. That's because the individuals respond to the group dynamic, and that's what we mean by self-organization. Complex conflict systems involve behavior that is non-rational because the phenomenon of self-organization acts on individuals and causes behavior that may not be intended.

Interests vs. Values

It also helps to think of conflict as being more about values than interests. In a negotiation, we are looking for alignment of interests, but a conflict is a perception of incompatible activities. That perception of incompatibility is driven, in part, by a difference in values. A few recent examples come to mind. In one situation, a regulatory body was examining the environmental impact of a potential transmission line, and one of the impacted Indigenous groups was protesting the proceedings. Both groups had the same interest; protecting the environment and minimizing any negative impacts. Their values, however, were quite different. The regulatory body was focused on the rule of law, fairness, and transparency when it came to holding large projects accountable for their impact. The Indigenous group was focused on the fact that they felt their internal territorial laws should take priority over the authority of the regulatory body. That was a clash of values, not interests.

In another example, we saw conflict over a pipeline expansion that was more about values than interests. The proponent argued that the expanded pipeline was the alternative that was most cost-effective, safe, and created less greenhouse gas (GHG) emissions. The protesting groups argued that trains were the best alternative because that infrastructure already existed. That conflict had little to do with interests because trains are more liable to spill, and they take a comparatively larger amount of energy and pollution to operate than a pipeline. Particularly, in this case, a pipeline that was only meant to expand existing capacity. This was a conflict over values, in which the protestors were unable to ethically support any type of pipeline expansion on principle. It was simply immoral to them.

The distinction between values and interests in the context of complex conflicts is essential for us because values are more prone to non-rational drivers than interests, and because complex conflicts are often rooted in values-based differences. Longstanding disputes are often based on fundamental values and world views, and they are more likely to resist resolution than interest-based disputes. That means they need to be handled differently than challenges based on miscommunication or misalignment. For example, disputes related to distribution will tend to revolve around interests and the allocation of resources, and gains and losses are tangible and measurable. However, in disputes related to values, the gains and losses are less clear and difficult to measure.

According to Schön & Rein [14], these types of disputes are "stubbornly resistant to resolution through the exercise of reason [and are] immune to resolution by appeal to facts." One conflict resolution approach is to remove any mismatch between needs and interests, but these types of disputes are "impervious to rationality"[15] and need to be handled differently. Bush & Folger[16] go so far as to suggest that effective mediation between parties with a value-based dispute requires nothing less than moral transformation on the part of the participants.

Good luck with that.

The question for us is, what can we change if our values are entrenched and immovable? It's a tall order to ask someone to change their values, but it might not be unreasonable to ask them to change how their values influence how they choose to act. More on that later.

Different Time Constraints

Negotiations also tend to be more time-constrained than conflicts. Negotiations are meant to be a fusing of interests, so they generally have time as an important constraint. This is especially true with financial negotiations because of the time value of money. If a negotiation can't be concluded within a specific timeframe, the potential financial benefits may not be realized. This is part of why most negotiations have a hard deadline. This forces the parties to prioritize and focus their efforts in a concerted fashion. On the other hand, complex conflicts may not always have a hard time constraint. With large projects, there are always milestones and roadmaps along the way, so this isn't a hard-and-fast rule. That said, we're not likely to hear something like, "We're going to have to wrap up this whole Palestinian/Israeli conflict by midnight next Wednesday, or the parties will walk away from the entire conflict." If only that were the case.

There may be discrete deadlines along the path of a conflict, but not necessarily for the entire conflict itself. Complex conflicts may come to an end, but rarely because the parties decided to adhere to an external deadline. The perception of incompatible activity will endure until those activities cease, or people change how their values drive their choices, not because of a calendar. Time constraints are a fundamental feature of most negotiations, but only one factor of many others for complex conflicts.

People vs. Issues

In negotiation training, they tell you to separate the people from the issues, but in a conflict, the people are the issues. That's part of what drives the rational vs. emotional differences. This has implications for strategy. In my work, I end up dividing my strategic efforts between big-picture issues and micro-relationships. We'll see a bit later that most conflicts can be boiled down to relationships between a few key individuals.

This is even more the case with more remote geographical areas, like small towns or remote territories, because the interpersonal relationships in remote areas have a more heightened sense of importance than they might have in a larger urban landscape. Interestingly enough, most large-scale projects are situated in these types of remote areas. Stakeholder engagement teams in those kinds of projects deserve everyone's respect.

If your strategy does not include interpersonal relationships between specific individuals at a micro level, you are virtually guaranteed to be missing a critical element of the situation. On a recent project, we spent a significant portion of our time focused on the dynamic relationships between a few related people whose complex family situation had a big impact on how the project unfolded. As we'll discuss shortly, people aren't just an important issue, they are THE issue.

Fight Different

Win vs. Lose-Lose

Another difference between negotiation and conflict is win-win versus lose-lose. In negotiation training, they teach us that we want to get a win-win solution so that both sides can come away with enough of an alignment of interests to enable them to agree; however, with conflicts that is often not possible. The fact that people have come to a point where they are in an open conflict means that you may have to aim for lose-lose as the best way forward.

This is partially because conflicts are usually about asserting enduring dominance and standing firm on immutable values. As we said, if a negotiation is unable to reach a mutually agreeable solution, one or more of the parties can walk away, and the negotiation ends. With those perceived incompatible activities, you can't walk away unless those incompatible activities cease. For a complex conflict to move from destructive to creative, both sides may end up feeling like they have lost something even though the result may be ultimately positive.

It's a matter of emphasis: prioritizing creative outcomes over positional success. Everybody may have to have to lose something in order to move forward, so that mindset is important when you're dealing with conflicts versus negotiations. It's similar to the other differences between negotiations and complex conflicts. A negotiation needs to be a net win for both sides, or they will walk away. If you wait for a conflict to be perceived as a win for everybody, it may never end.

Agreement vs. Creative Engagement

The next difference between negotiations and conflicts is the intended outcome. We touched on this briefly in the definition section. When dealing with complex conflicts, that's not as easy as you might think because the end is not always clear.

Spoiler alert; there is no such thing as resolution in a complex conflict. This may also be what can help you distinguish the difference between a conflict and a complex one. It might help to think of it this way; a complicated conflict may be resolvable, but a complex one isn't.

Given what we have learned about conflicts so far, resolution may be the wrong way of looking at what we are trying to accomplish in the first place. We've discovered that complex conflicts start and continue because the participants have a perception of incompatible activities.

That perception is informed by their values and their non-rational side as much, or more, than their rational side. This leads to the Coherence Trap, where their need to make sense of things outstrips their ability to, or interest in, factor in all the relevant information about other conflict participants. The Coherence Trap leads to dried-up patterns of interaction between participants, which then pushes the conflict in a destructive direction.

It is difficult to create anything when you are working with faulty or incomplete information because you can't think about things you refuse to see in the first place. The very idea that we can resolve a specific conflict speaks to our desire to control outcomes that we cannot hope to control. Based on what we have been learning, the objective of our work as Focal Thinkers might not be to resolve a conflict (since that's out of our control), but rather to create winning conditions for our conflicts to be the kind of creative processes that will help us get from the current state to the desired state; the bridge from what is to what should be. According to our model so far, the path to ensuring the conflict is creative and not destructive involves reintroducing a healthy level of information transfer between the participants. The dried-up patterns need to be rejuvenated. Old prejudices and constricting frames need to be replaced with new ways of thinking about other participants, and even about ourselves. This will become the focus of our Focal Thinking efforts, and in how we implement this at work. Bringing new life to negative patterns of interaction will be the key to accomplishing what needs to be done.

That is different from negotiations, which are focused on gaining mutually beneficial agreement between people in the near term. The results are meant to endure, but the negotiation itself is supposed to end. Like high and low tide, locked in everlasting struggle, a complex conflict may never reach an agreement, but as long as they're still engaging with all their might, something productive might come of it. All we can do is try to make that happen, one participant at a time.

Wrap-Up and What's Next

In this chapter, we covered the important differences between negotiations and conflicts. Complex conflicts often have more participants, are driven more by emotion and values, and are not necessarily time-constrained. It can be more helpful to think of complex conflicts in terms of getting to lose-lose instead of win-win, and the process is more about creative engagement than getting agreement.

Next, we're going to talk about an important source of the Coherence Trap: how participants frame themselves, others, and the issues involved.

Reality vs. Frames

When people fall into the Coherence Trap, they put blinders on to reduce the discomfort that comes from disorienting complexity. One way people put blinders on is to frame things in a way that makes sense to them. This is a very important topic in the research on complex conflicts, so you'll find it helpful to go a bit deeper on this.

In this context, framing is the idea that we build pictures or narratives of ourselves and others involved in the conflict to make sense of their behavior and to signal who we are to other participants. Davis & Lewicki define frames as

> "abstractions, perceptions, interpretations of a situation. They cannot be seen, but they are the way we all see the world, define what is important, organize information, etc. We can infer others' frames by asking them directly what they think is going on, by listening to their communication, and by watching their behavior."[17]

With frames, external factors can influence the perceptions and attitudes of conflict participants. For example, culture, norms, beliefs, professional position, organizational policies, and how big and powerful your organization is may all influence how a participant frames his or her identity and values in relation to the conflict. Framing helps people solidify their own subjective perceptions of the conflict. And since the very definition of conflict is rooted in perception, that's no small thing. Like any other oversimplification, if we leave frames unchallenged, they're going to increase people's resistance to engaging.

It needs to be said that there is absolutely nothing wrong with frames. They can give us purpose, focus, and the ability to make decisions in what might be an otherwise overwhelmingly complex situation. The issue is not in the use of the frame; it's in the misuse. When we rely on our chosen frames as a replacement for thinking, observing, or genuinely responding to counterfactual information when it comes at us, that's essentially putting on the same blinders that lead to the Coherence Trap. That's what we need to watch out for as practitioners in the art and science of Focal Thinking.

Let's see if we can get a sense of what frames are and how they impact behavior. Davis & Lewicki[18] provide some examples of frames that relate specifically to complex environmental conflicts.

Identity Frame

The Identity frame refers to how conflict participants choose to self-identify. For example, if I see myself as working for social justice to protect the environment, I am going to behave in a specific way. I will make certain decisions, I will express myself to others in a certain way, I will join certain groups, and I will make sure to stand firmly on values rooted in what I learn and adopt from other like-minded people. And I will feel fantastic doing so because it's a great way to authentically live out my values.

Similarly, if I identify myself as a protector of Indigenous rights, I will behave and express myself to the world in a way that is consistent with that set of values. The same is also true if I chose to identify myself as a land developer, with values rooted in turning raw land into productive land that can provide people with houses and the ability to trade with each other to make a living for themselves and their loved ones. Each of these identities is intensely personal and closely held, and each of these identities can either mutually overlap or live in direct conflict. The problem happens when we refuse to entertain counterfactual information that puts our identity in jeopardy. For example, that land developer is going to need to be open to the fact that the Indigenous group impacted by the development has years of historical mistreatment, and they may not be interested in making money off the project because they have other priorities. When new information comes at us, if we don't embrace it voraciously, it means we're probably at risk of getting stuck in our own identity frame.

Characterization Frame

The Characterization frame refers to how participants categorize other participants and their perceived beliefs and values. This is the other side of the identity frame coin. It's not how I characterize myself; it's how I characterize you. When we frame others, it can help us make sense of where they're coming from, but like any frame, this can be open to abuse. When I refuse to hear what another is saying because I've characterized them in a way that's convenient for me, that's a frame-based blinder I'm putting on myself. That's also called stereotyping. If I can't listen to the points being made by a person because they're wearing a certain hat, coming from a specific region of the world, or looking a certain way, I'm probably missing a lot of other nuances and important information around me. Welcome to the Coherence Trap, courtesy of your own frame. Enjoy the view.

Conflict Management Frame

The Conflict Management frame refers to preferences for how conflicts should be managed. Not everybody believes that disputes should be handled formally. Not everyone agrees that conflicts over things like land use, for example, should be handled within a highly procedural regulatory framework. Some would prefer to buck the system and obstruct the process. Some would argue that once you're using Roberts Rules of Order, you have essentially killed any opportunity to have constructive, non-adversarial engagement. Others prefer to have the certainty of the process so they know what they're getting into, and they can be sure of how to prepare. These differences of perspective change and color how people choose to participate in a conflict, and they often go directly to how much they respect the rule of law in their society. Again, there's nothing wrong with that *per se*, until it turns into self-imposed blinders that prevent people from hearing the thoughts and opinions of others.

Fact-Finding Frame

The Fact-Finding frame refers to the way technical information is perceived by participants, including experts and non-experts. Data are not facts until we decide what to do with the information they contain. Who gets to decide that? Do we only listen to so-called experts? What about people who are only experts in how they feel about a proposed project? What is the role of science, and whose science are we talking about? For example, is it more scientific to count polar bears by flying over a territory, or by listening to the people who have been living on that land for millennia? What if the flying scientists think the bears are in trouble, but the locals are seeing more than ever? The role of the decider-of-facts is a critical part of any dispute, and how you see that role will definitely influence your perspective on the data that comes in. The question is whether you'll be open to a wide range of data that might not fit your particular frame.

We've seen this play out recently with the COVID-19 pandemic. Subject matter experts know the disease but not policy development. They're not necessarily trained in balancing other social needs. When we over-rely on immunologists, it's no wonder policy decisions ignore the impact of isolation, economic devastation, and other predictable outcomes of the lockdown.

Social Control Frame

The Social Control frame refers to perceptions of how decisions regarding social issues should be made. This is similar to the Conflict Management frame, but it relates more to a broader range of social decision making that might go beyond the specific conflict. Is the government the only group that can make decisions that impact broader society? What part of the government should that even be? What is the role of civil society and non-governmental organizations? A good example is the expanding role of energy regulators. Initially, they were set up to be enforcers of regulations. However, because governments in North America had largely abdicated their role in facilitating social engagement, many regulatory bodies now have to play the role of social convener and engagement facilitator. The rule cops are not always the best-equipped to play that role, so there's been an adjustment period. Depending on how you see the role of social engineering, you may frame this matter differently than others. Will that blind you to alternatives, or will you let that be just part of a more robust way of thinking?

Power Frame

The Power frame refers to the dynamic of power between disputants. Some people will see a conflict through the lens of power imbalances. It's always good to make sure that those who have less power or are otherwise marginalized have a voice in any complex conflict. Too often, they go under-represented and left out of the final resolution. That leads to incomplete solutions and simmering resentments. As always, the key is to make sure that relative power is an important consideration but not the driving force. The powerful should not always get their way just because they're powerful. But just because someone is marginalized does not give their perspective more virtue, simply because they need support in participating in the process. The central issue is whether this frame puts comfortable blinders on that prevent you from being aware of details you might otherwise miss.

Risk Frame

The Risk frame refers to the perception of risk around costs, gains or losses, benefits, and advantages. This revolves around who should bear the risks involved in a conflict situation. Any project or initiative will have risks, and how you choose to see the world may drive who you think should be bearing those risks. A large organization trying to create an infrastructure project will continuously have their eye on the interest rate because as the cost of capital fluctuates, so do the risks associated with their financing strategy. This is the weak flank that anti-project groups will exploit by clogging the process or slowing things down because every day of delay adds to the cost of the project. The hope will be that the proponent gives up and walks away if it takes too long. From a policy perspective, the question for society is; if they want infrastructure to support their way of life, should the proponent bear all that risk alone? And if not, how will you re-distribute that risk? How you answer questions along those lines will inform how you frame the risk, and that will drive different perspectives and choices.

It's fair to say that the more objective and rational the matter at hand, the less that frames are going to influence what goes on. If negotiations are more rational and calculated, it will stand to reason that they may be more open to a robust reality than conflicting participants. It's also true that when relevant data comes to light in a negotiation, there's no hiding from it or pretending it's something it's not. Hard data are pretty difficult to dispute when the goal is to align interests. Their meaning and what you do with them can be open to question, but the data themselves are not something that can be easily framed away to obscurity. That's not necessarily true in complex conflicts when there are so many issues that are open to interpretation based on the perspective of the participants.

Framing is a great example of the lengths conflict participants will go to attempt to make sense of the complexity they face. To the extent that they prevent participants from genuinely engaging in robust patterns of behavior based on a full range of information, frames will be another path to the Coherence Trap.

Wrap-Up and What's Next

Hopefully, you now have a better understanding of the nature of complex conflicts, especially how they differ from negotiations. At the root of the difference is the level of uncertainty, and that drives a number of the other differences:

- Different Sizes
- Rational vs. Emotional
- Interests vs. Values
- Different time constraints
- People vs. Issues
- Win-Win vs. Win-Lose
- Agreement vs. Creative Engagement
- Reality vs. Frames

Now we're going to go a little bit deeper into the science behind what we've been talking about, and show how that points to some more practical ways we can avoid the Coherence Trap, get to a mindset of ROR, and enable us to show strategic leadership by knowing what to do next, and why to do it.

SECTION THREE: NATURE IS THE TEACHER

So far, we've talked a lot about the problem but not the solution. It's time to start getting to the practical part. To do that, you're going to want to know that the solutions are rooted in solid science, so this section of the book is going to talk about what practical things we can learn from the science on the topic of complex conflicts. I'm going to keep it easy to understand, so don't worry about getting bogged down in academic jargon. Some extraordinary minds have gone on before us, and we're going to take a minute to cherry-pick the good stuff before we lay out the roadmap.

Einstein reportedly said, "Look deep into nature, and then you will understand everything better." That hit home for me as I was doing my original research because all this talk of complexity and birds and uncertainty sounded a lot like something that was part of nature. The science points in the same direction: complex conflicts behave very much like other natural systems. If that's true, then we should be able to learn a lot from how science makes sense of those natural systems and apply it to complex conflicts.

Here's how this section is organized. The first part will be a quick primer on how to use science to make sense of things. The second part will talk about the overall theory from social psychology that makes the connection between complex systems and complex human conflicts. Third, we will look at a conflict approach from the world of engineering that will help clarify where we need to focus our attention in the midst of all the chaos. Next, we will look at a slightly different type of logic that will help us use complexity to our advantage. These are the streams of scientific thought that I mashed together as I developed my research, and the combination of them led me to develop the underlying science behind Focal Thinking. Lastly, we will tie it together and summarize what this all is telling us about complex conflicts and why it can be difficult for us to incorporate this way of thinking into our approach.

Sensemaking

Look deep into nature, and then you will understand everything better.

Albert Einstein

When we talked about the Coherence Trap, I said that a big part of the problem when dealing with complex conflicts is rooted in our own thinking. Our natural need for coherence works against us when we bump up against something with that much uncertainty because it encourages us to grasp for what we are comfortable understanding rather than the full scope of reality. We need to make that natural need for coherence work for us, not against us.

With something as messy and challenging as a complex conflict, it's important to have the kind of tools that will help us make sense of it all. Part of the challenge lies in the fact that most folks are not trained to think about big, messy things like this in an organized, systematic way. It will be helpful to spend a bit of time on a few new tools to help you with that, so a little bit of background theory will help put the practical part in context.

We talked about what can happen when we apply negotiation techniques to a complex conflict, and how that part of our training can end up getting in the way. There's a similar gap in our training that we're going to cover now, and it's rooted in our understanding of science itself.

In most of our education, we are taught to use inductive reasoning, probabilities, and experiments to make sense of the world around us. For example, we try to reduce any kind of risk before we act, and then we act in hopes that our calculations were correct. We experiment using "the" scientific method as if experimentation was the only established scientific approach available to us. (It's not.) In reality, however, conflicts don't lend themselves to this kind of approach. When trying to make sense of a conflict, we can't simply pause a conflict in time, experiment with it to understand its workings, start it back up again, and try to predict or influence where it will all end. That's part of why complicated conflicts continue to challenge us. There is a better way; using scientific tools designed to analyze complex natural systems.

As we learn how to make sense of complex conflicts, our approach to knowing where to focus our attention will be critical since we can't use the usual experimental methods. This can be uncomfortable because we crave certainty and predictability, and as a leader, advisor, or participant, you'll be expected to have a crystal ball to foresee what will likely happen.

Complex systems can't be predicted, but they can be understood if you know where to focus your attention. Our approach to knowing where to focus determines the threshold at which we will accept what we observe as being reality. Facts are not truth; they are data points that we interpret. That interpretation should be clearly explained before we start observing so that when the facts roll in, we know how to arrange them into truth.

For our purposes, there are some implications to this. First, we need to understand that making sense of complex conflicts will not be a one-time event; it will unfold over time. Any truth claim we make must account for the fact that everything can and likely will change over time. Making sense of complexity is like putting our foot in Heraclitus' river. He was the Greek philosopher who said you can never step into the same river twice because its constant motion means it's always changing. It might look the same, but don't be fooled. That water is entirely different than it was a few minutes ago. When we remember our murmuration of starlings, that certainly rings true. That system is never the same twice. Same birds, different formation.

Second, any claims to truth about complex conflicts should account for the fact that the reality we are examining happens between the ears of those participating in the conflict. Remember, conflict is the *perception* of incompatible activities. The relational processes occur at the individual and group level, but the truth we are looking for happens in the minds of participants. Because conflict happens in the mind, we have to focus on what's going on in the minds of those participating. This means we have to be able to speak to the impact of underlying motivations and the murky world of ever-changing human thought and emotion. If we're not getting into people's heads, we're not doing our job as Focal Thinkers.

Lastly, we need to focus on the fact that we are part of the conflict ourselves, so we need to account for what we bring to it as well. What we observe is often changed by our act of observing it. In our case, we will not be observing as an experimenter might, and we're definitely not going to be a neutral third party that has no impact on the conflict. Everyone involved has skin in the game. Everyone has an objective for the outcome. There is nothing wrong with having an agenda or required outcome. That is to be expected. Nobody is completely neutral. Nobody is agnostic. We will just need to acknowledge the impact of our own participation and openly declare our own perspective.

When we talk about making sense of something, we're talking about *bringing meaning to what we observe.* We see a thing and decide what it means to us. When we talk about "sensemaking," we're talking about the process by which we attach that meaning. Making sense of complex conflicts, therefore, is going to be about how we understand what we observe when we look at complex conflicts, and then what we choose to do with that. This is important for Focal Thinking because it not only requires us to think, but it also requires us to think about our own thinking; to observe our own approach to how we bring meaning to what we are seeing. Thinking about thinking, or "metacognition," is a vital component to our ability to make sense of complexity.

As leaders, advisors, and conflict participants who are trying to make sense of complex conflicts, we may need to change our way of thinking about them, but how do we accomplish that? How will we know if it is working? Here's how: we're going to make sense of complex conflicts the way scientists do.

Wrap-Up and What's Next

When we deal with anything complex, i.e. something where the outcome is impossible to predict, we have to accept a high level of ambiguity. This is not something we are generally comfortable with because we want to understand something before we act on it. That fundamental human instinct is what helps us survive as a species, but it is also what makes it difficult for us to operate in ambiguous environments like complex conflicts. Our sensemaking goal, therefore, is to be able to navigate in spite of ambiguity; to be able to take action even if we do not have all the answers immediately at hand. This is the challenge faced by those who need to spark action today when the future is unknowable.

Now it's time to start digging into some of the practical approaches others have used to enable themselves to move forward in the face of ambiguity and uncertainty so that we can stand on the shoulders of giants.

Nonlinear Dynamical Systems

So far, we touched on the fact that a big part of what creates complexity (i.e. uncertain outcomes) in conflicts is non-rational decision-making that makes a conflict behave like a self-organizing system. In fact, they behave as what scientists call a "nonlinear dynamical system" or NDS. They call it "dynamical" because that's a term that relates to the mathematical subject of dynamics. We'll use that term when referring to the theory, but we'll also use "dynamic" in the usual sense of something that's always changing.

Simply put, NDS theory describes precisely the kind of behavior we observe in complex conflicts. If we think of conflicts as an NDS, that opens up a whole world of opportunities in terms of finding a way to guide us to that all-important Release, Observe, Revisit that will enable us to get out of the Coherence Trap. Here's how this relates to complex conflicts.

System

First of all, conflict behavior can be explained as if it were a system, which is the outcome of patterns of interaction between its internal components. It's got a boundary to it, and we can observe it's inner workings. With our starlings, we can tell what is flock and what is sky, and we know the birds pay attention to each other with some sort of organized rules. Another example is a school of fish, which moves in a similar pattern. As you would expect, each fish in the school adjusts to the fish in its immediate vicinity, and there is no guiding leader controlling the overall school. And yet, the group holds together and accomplishes what it needs to; hunting, feeding, predator protection, etc. In the same way, with a complex conflict, we can tell who's in and who's out, and we know that people and groups interact with each other.

The benefit of treating complex conflicts as a system is that doing so enables us to focus on the patterns of interaction between participants while simultaneously keeping an eye on the overall state of the conflict. This is incredibly powerful, and using NDS as our chosen type of systems theory adds even more specificity to the explanatory power of the theory.

Nonlinear

When systems are nonlinear, the inputs are not proportionate to the outputs. The effort we put into a conflict to bring about some sort of change is rarely consistent nor proportional to the result we get. Intuitively this makes sense. Years and years of effort to resolve a conflict may result in no change to the conflict itself whatsoever, but one small action can suddenly spark enormous upheaval. This is why, later in the book, we will see that it helps to think in terms of small nudges as you influence a conflict. In a nonlinear system, those seemingly little steps can have a big impact.

Dynamic

When systems are static, they do not change over time. Complex systems, on the other hand, are dynamic because they are in a constant state of change. Change is one of their defining factors. This quality brings a high degree of uncertainty when examining and making sense of complex conflicts, and the process of decision making under uncertainty has been studied extensively, particularly by Kahneman & Tversky.[19] These tools are available to us as we look at how to make sense of complex conflicts.

Emergence

Another important idea that comes with NDS is emergence. Emergence is an academic term conveying the idea that we will not know what is going to happen until after it has happened. Your finance department will hate that, but the concept of emergence takes on a vital role in the analysis of human conflict because conflict itself is a result of ongoing complex interactions. Individual points in a conflict's timeframe won't tell us much in and of themselves because they cannot fully explain the patterns that emerge. This is critical to wrap our minds around when we are trying to make sense of complex conflicts. It means we can't predict a specific outcome, and we need to focus our attention on the result of the patterns of interaction we see in the conflict. We have to pay attention to what is going on inside the minds of participants, and then wait and see what the outcome of their interactions is going to be. As we will see shortly, this will also connect to how we're going to measure all this, since the outcome of those interactions will only emerge over time.

Wrap-Up and What's Next

We're just scratching the surface here, but NDS theory is a very powerful way to explain what we observe in complex conflicts. The parallels with other natural systems are striking, and this gives us a very helpful context for us to start making sense of the mayhem. In doing my original research, I found, however, that two other approaches to understanding and resolving conflicts that were consistent with NDS and a bit more down-to-earth in their practical application. Next, we're going to talk about those two approaches, from the disciplines of systems engineering and design thinking, and see how they will help us complete the picture.

The Graph Model for Conflict Resolution

The second aspect of science that I incorporated into my research was the Graph Model for Conflict Resolution (GMCR), which was developed at the systems engineering department at the University of Waterloo.[20] The GMCR is an agent-based modeling system that examines the decision-making priorities of each individual involved in a conflict, estimates the next decision that they are likely to make based on risk tolerance and how influenced they are by other parties, and then projects all the possible conflict outcomes based on all the possible decisions. For me, it was important to use the GMCR because it helped me learn how to focus on the participants that matter the most. When you try and add too many into the model it becomes unwieldy and impossible to use, which, of course, is very much like reality. If you have too many factors, you can't make any real decisions. Using the GMCR helped me focus on where the real power in a conflict lies. More on that later.

The GMCR also makes use of a scientific methodology other than experimentation. As we've already noted, you can't experiment on a conflict because you can't just stop it, poke around in its inner workings, and fire it back up again to see what happens. Since a complex conflict is dynamic, time is a critical element of the process, and you can't just stop time. One useful methodology in these scenarios is called agent-based modeling (ABM), and GMCR is an example of that methodology.

If you have ever played the game The Sims, you will understand the basis of ABM. If you think back to the murmuration of starlings or the school of fish, ABM uses computer simulations to recreate those kinds of natural phenomena by programming rules for how each unit will behave and interact with all the others. Scientists use this type of simulation to examine the systemic impacts of small changes in the patterns of interaction. Biologists and environmental scientists use this to model predator-prey interactions. City planners use it to model traffic patterns and population flows. Social scientists use it to model conflict interactions, and this is of particular interest to us.

ABM not only handles data that emerge over time, it effectively compresses the impact of time within the simulated environment. Part of the value of ABM lies in the unexpected results that come from being able to fast-forward the effects of time and look for any counterintuitive findings.

ABM is important for a few reasons. Its importance to social psychology and theory building reminds us of the importance of emergence and generative analysis. That is to say, we watch and observe first, and then we evaluate the outcome. Methodologies like ABM remind us that we can't expect to get all the answers at once, but we can make progress. Relentless progress. It is also important because it reminds us of the power of micro-interactions. When we change one small aspect of how the modeled agents interact, it can have an enormous impact on the overall system. This is important to remember as we start looking at Focal Thinking and the process by which we start making sense of specific conflicts. The other important aspect of ABM is that it serves as a reminder to hold the system we are examining loosely. When we get too caught up in the end results and lose focus on the patterns of individual interaction that we can actually influence, we will start looking for the kind of intellectual shortcuts that create the very Coherence Trap we are trying to avoid.

The GMCR is a type of ABM simulation that looks at the impact of decisions made in the context of a conflict. Each participant in the simulation is assumed to have a series of preferences, options, and priorities. The software projects the various possible outcomes of the decisions that agents might make. Those decisions are guided by levels of risk tolerance and interaction with the other participants, including the well-known Nash equilibrium (which you may recall from the movie *A Beautiful Mind*).

Even if you ignore the emotionally charged and constantly changing nature of conflicts, part of the challenge to making sense of them is sorting out where the source of the conflict actually lies. The more complicated the conflict, the more challenging this is. One benefit of using a methodology like the GMCR, or any other agent-based model, is that it forces the researcher to boil the conflict down to its most basic elements. While that exercise helps one build a formal model, it can help one get to the heart of the conflict regardless of whether you use the information for a model. That is part of why Focal Thinking is such a robust approach. It does not require software or anything but information and your own beautiful mind.

Wrap-Up and What's Next

NDS helps provide an overall context for why conflicts become complex and the importance of focusing effort on patterns of interaction between participants. The GMCR helps by showing the insane amount of permutations and combinations and ramifications that come from trying to account for the decision-making priorities of too many participants, forcing us to focus on the ones that actually matter. The process of deciding which ones to pay attention to and which to (temporarily) ignore is what helped me create the idea of Focal Thinking in the first place. We can never hope to model an entire complex conflict, but we certainly can focus on the participants that matter, which will help us focus our efforts on changing the patterns of interaction.

Next, we will talk about the ways design thinking can help us approach the creation and implementation of those new patterns.

Design Thinking

Once we know that we have to focus on patterns of interaction between participants, we need to decide how to approach the creation and implementation of those new patterns. That's where design thinking can help us. Design thinking is usually associated with situations where people are interested in, or at least willing to, be collaborative with each other, so that's not something we'd typically associate with conflicts. But it works.

There are many approaches to design thinking, including those from David Kelley, founder of the Hasso Plattner Institute of Design at Stanford (known as the "d.school"), and Dr. Roger Martin from his time at the Rotman School of Management. These institutions, and those like them, have been able to apply their design thinking process collaboratively with other disciplines like business, law, medicine, engineering, humanities, social sciences, and others.

It's important to note that we're not talking about graphic design or interior design. We're talking about design in the largest possible sense of the word. Whenever we develop something new, we are designing. Design is said to be "normative," meaning that it looks at what exists today and says what that should be in the future. The process of how we get from what *is* to what *should be* is the process of design thinking. In our case, we are looking at a complex conflict as what is, and we're trying to get it to the point where it should be in the future. Design thinkers are well-known for their ability to take action in the face of ambiguity and uncertainty, so it stands to reason that we can learn something from them.

Different Types of Logic

As we noted in the introduction, when we apply straight-line thinking to a chaotic world, we miss some vital nuances along the way. Part of what encourages our straight-line thinking is how we're trained to think. We talk about thinking "logically," meaning how we get from A to B in a sequential, orderly fashion. That works perfectly well when we have all the information we need, but it doesn't help us in situations

56

of ambiguity. We need a type of logic that lets us get from A to Z when everything in between is unknown and unknowable. Fortunately, there is more than one kind of logic, and there happens to be a type of logic that's perfectly suited to our purpose. It also happens to be the same type of logic that design thinkers use to work their magic. It's called "abductive" logic.

Different approaches to logical inference work for different types of observations. Here's a helpful analogy. Imagine that we are standing on the banks of a wide river. The water is turbulent from all the rocks hidden under the surface. It is the kind of river that you could imagine crossing on foot if you had to, but you'd get a bit wet. Now imagine that we want to find a way to get to the other side. Our pattern of thinking will determine how we might approach the challenge. Here are three types of reasoning that we might apply.

The first type of logical reasoning we might use is *deductive*. With deductive inferences, the outcome is a logical certainty. The classic example of deductive reasoning is "A = B, B = C, therefore A = C." In the case of our river crossing, deductive reasoning would be like a bridge that we might build to the other side. That bridge would be made of solid stone, concrete, or steel, and would be wide enough to accommodate pretty much anything you'd want to drive over it. There is no question about our ability to cross that bridge and get to the other side. It is a logical certainty that we will get across. Deductive reasoning is a useful way of thinking when we need to make sense of ideas, arguments, or facts that have a logical sequence. When presented with these, we organize our thinking in a way that will help us prove or disprove the validity of the arguments, positions, or assertions. Deduction works well to organize our thinking about thoughts and ideas.

The world around us, however, doesn't always lend itself to logical certainties, and that is where *inductive* reasoning can be helpful. Inductive reasoning is useful for logical probabilities. A classic example is: "Every time I do X, Y occurs. Therefore, if I do X under the same conditions, Y will probably also occur." To get us to the other side of our river, this wouldn't be a solid stone bridge because that's too certain. It might be something more like a catapult. We can make calculations of the force required to launch someone the distance of the river, the angle from which they would need to take off, the amount of cushioning or the size of the net required at the other side to catch them, the ability of a person to withstand all those pressures, etc. Based on all our calculations, we would do our best to increase the probability of success of getting ourselves over safely. Our success will be dependent on our ability to reduce the probability of catastrophe.

Much of how we approach business planning is based on inductive logic. We identify an objective, and we plan for ways to increase our probability of success and reduce our probability of failure. In most cases, we take no action until we conclude that we have collectively— through all our organizational processes—identified and mitigated all the foreseeable risks. Once everyone involved agrees that there is a sufficient likelihood of success, we will proceed. Induction works well when we can identify and mitigate all possible permutations and combinations of risk.

The world around us does not always lend itself to situations where we can identify all the possible risks at the outset, and that's where *abductive* reasoning can help. Sometimes we have to make decisions and take action when there is no possible way to know the risks because we don't have all the facts, and we never will. We can't possibly identify all unknowns, and yet we still have to make a decision now. A classic example: "I see that Z just occurred, and I think A is the best possible explanation for that." In other words, you see the outcome first, and then try to figure out how it came about. You can see why that works well for designing something new because you can see the result you want, but you don't always know how you're going to do it until you get started. Kolko put this another way: "Abduction is a logical way of considering inference or 'best guess' leaps."[21] Designers, planners, and strategists use abductive reasoning because it effectively addresses the types of challenges they face where they know the desired impact, but they do not yet know how to achieve it.[22]

Back to our river analogy, there is a Chinese idiom that explains it well. Loosely translated, it means to cross a river by feeling your way, one stone at a time. This approach is useful when your outcome is not a logical certainty, and when you can't possibly foresee all the risks in taking action. By starting with a small step in the right direction and continually recalibrating your progress, you can get to the other side of the river. There is no guarantee of success. The path you end up taking will not be a straight line. You may need to double back and try something in a slightly different way. You may need to collaborate with others to help you, particularly if you do not have the full range of skills required yourself.

The key to abductive reasoning lies in the process itself. Abduction is the process of synthesizing incomplete information. It emerges as part of an ongoing process of interaction between the elements of a system, and it unfolds over time. You can immediately see the parallels with a complex system, and why our model fits with this methodology. Merçay & Borrie noted that when it comes to conflict systems, generalized rules have limited predictive power, "not because social interactions cannot be understood [but] because events unfold in dramatically different ways depending on very small changes: the unpredictability is ingrained."[23]

Design Thinking, Explained

Again, we're not talking about graphic design or interior design here. Design is much larger than that. We're talking about the process of creating what we think should exist out of what does exist. Harold Nelson (The Design Way)[24] explains it this way: "Design is the action of bringing something new and desired into existence—a proactive stance that resolves or dissolves problematic situation. It is a compound of routine, adaptive and design expertise brought to bear on complex dynamic situations."

Hmm. "Complex dynamic situations," you say? That sounds like exactly what we're trying to accomplish.

Design thinking is a practical expression of abductive reasoning. It is used by innovators, engineers, lawyers, planners, and other designers who take what is and create what should be. In many ways, that is the underlying root of most conflict in the first place—the creation of something new from what currently exists, creating a perception of incompatible activities—so there might be things we can learn regarding how they accomplish this.

Design thinking is about the process of how we apply the abstract notion of crossing-the-river-one-stone-at-a-time abduction to a real-world challenge: Solving problems and making decisions that guide us to a solution when the steps to achieve it are murky at best. In a moment, we will discuss how and why this type of approach is particularly useful in making sense of complex conflicts, and it will also provide some guidance to how we choose to influence the patterns of interaction within a conflict. There are many different descriptions of this process, and I would encourage you to go deeper into this topic at your earliest opportunity. For our purposes, the steps can be broken down by using the example of Apollo 13.

While in orbit around the moon, the Apollo 13 spacecraft had a catastrophic failure ("Houston, we have a problem.") that vented most of their oxygen into space, leaving barely enough to get the astronauts home alive. The engineering team on the ground in Houston had to find a way to fix the problem using only what was on board the ship. The process they used was a classic example of design thinking. I'll explain these stages in order, but the process is not necessarily linear or sequential. Think of it more like a circular track that you can enter at any point. The goal is not to start at one point and finish at another; the goal of this process is to keep running on the track until you are in shape. It is a marathon, not a sprint. And it happens to be in a crooked line, where you will need to change direction a hundred times on a moment's notice.

The most critical stage is defining the problem. A problem clarified is a problem half-solved, as the saying goes. If we are going to cross our river, we need to know precisely where we are headed, or we won't be able to tell if we're making progress as we feel our way across, stone by stone. This is particularly true in situations where we can easily get lost along the way. That is the biggest challenge with abductive reasoning. If we were walking over a bridge (deduction) or catapulting ourselves over (induction), we wouldn't need to give any thought to where we were headed. When we're feeling our way along the river, we run the real danger of losing sight of the other side. This is why people who use this type of approach spend a great deal of effort being clear on what they are trying to accomplish because it's easy to get sidetracked.

However, problem definition is not as easy as you would think, because people often confuse *problem clarification* with *roadblock identification*. The difference between the two is simple. A clarified problem has the seeds of its own solution, but an identified roadblock doesn't. In the case of the Apollo 13 crew, they barely had enough oxygen to survive the trip home. That is not a clarification of the problem; that is simply an identification of the roadblock. After spending some time on the issue, the engineers at Houston realized that the real problem was less about insufficient oxygen and more about a surplus of carbon dioxide created by the astronauts' breathing. Once they were clear on the actual problem, the team could then go about trying to solve it, and that is exactly how they got the crew home alive. They created a CO2 scrubber that removed the excess CO2 from the air on the ship, using what they had available on board.

The Right Future

The key to making sure you are clarifying a problem and not merely identifying a roadblock has four parts. First, you need to be aware of whether the problem, as stated, will create the future you want. Once the engineers realized the issue was CO2, then they knew that was the key to the solution. But in order to accomplish that, you need to be aware of the impact of what you are doing on the people who matter. That was obvious in the case of Apollo 13 because the astronauts were either going to live or die. But in most design challenges, the outcome isn't clear. As an architect plans a habitable space, an engineer envisions the design of a bridge, a community planner scopes out the needs of a neighborhood, or an industrial designer creates a medical device, the needs of the end-user drive the decision making. Their problems become the focus of the design solution. This is why design thinkers spend so much time and effort thinking about what meaning their solution will bring to the lives of the people impacted. That meaning then helps drive the problem to be addressed. Jørn Utson, the architect of the Sydney Opera House, was known to spend a great deal of time just thinking about the lives of the people that would be inhabiting his spaces, long before he put pen to paper.[25] His focus was on what the space would mean to people, and his designs were shaped to solve the problem of what element of that meaning was missing from their lives. Klaus Krippendorff's book, *The Semantic Turn*[26], is a manifesto on the importance of understanding meaning as part of the design process and is highly recommended if you want to go deeper on this topic.

Get All the Inputs

The second stage along the design thinking crooked path is making sure you have all the available inputs at hand. Design thinking is a process of synthesizing what currently exists into what should exist in the future. But we can't get to *what should be* until we are clear on *what is*. In the case of Apollo 13, once the engineers realized that the problem was CO_2, they had to collect everything available to them on board the spaceship that could be used to create a CO_2 scrubber. They quickly grabbed examples of what the astronauts had on board and piled it all on a large table. What they eventually discovered was the need to (literally) make a square peg fit into a round hole. Using all the bits and pieces they had available, they were able to cobble together a device that removed enough CO_2 from the ambient air to enable the astronauts to survive. This process is also known as *bricolage*: creation from a diverse range of available things. If they didn't have all the parts available at the same time, they might not have succeeded. You can't synthesize what you can't see. If a critical element of the overall puzzle is missing from the beginning, your chances of success are reduced. For those not trying to necessarily save astronauts, these initial inputs might include things like timing constraints, budgets, physical hurdles, or critical elements of what the end-user needs for you to create meaning. Everything needs to be on the table at the beginning, or your design solution will miss the mark.

Create & Evaluate

The next waypoint in the design thinking circle is the creative & evaluative process. Being creative is like building muscles. You don't build muscles by lifting weights; you build them by resting after you have lifted weights. Similarly, you're not creative when you are trying to be, you're creative after you have identified the problem, you have all the inputs to synthesize, and you go off and think of something unrelated. The best ideas happen in the shower, on a walk, or while you are doing something completely different because the creative synthesis occurs subconsciously. This is also why brainstorming is not useful for creativity. Teams are very good at problem clarification and evaluation of options, but they're not great for idea generation. The best approach is for folks to think on their own, or possibly in pairs if you have the right partner, to develop options for how to solve the problem using the inputs that you have available. Then you regroup with the larger team to see what might work and refine your approach based on the team's input. The Apollo 13 engineers went off on their own for the most part once they knew the real problem was excess

CO2, and then they would come back together as a team to evaluate the prototype solution options. To go deeper on this topic, I highly recommend *Where Good Ideas Come From* by Steven Johnson.[27]

Exit Ramp

The last waypoint on the design thinking path is the exit ramp. At some point, you need to stop prototyping and start putting the solution to use. I recall an interview with a Pixar Studios executive who said that they never actually finish a movie, they just release it. When using abductive reasoning to design solutions, you could, theoretically, continue the tweaking and refining process forever. I am an amateur (very amateur) music producer in my non-existent spare time, and the biggest challenge I face is knowing when to just stop tinkering with the dang snare drum compression and move on. Design solutions are rarely finished; they bump up against the cold reality of timelines, budgets, or (as in the case of Apollo 13) life-or-death choices. Knowing when you are finished is often the most challenging part of the design thinking process. This is where the importance of your clearly articulated problem is vital. If you get that part right, the exit ramp is easier to recognize. That is part of why this process is circular and not linear. You may well find that the solution helps you clarify the problem you should have been trying to solve in the first place, in which case you can re-state the problem and carry on. You may have thought you were aiming for the sandy part of the river's other side, but once you got closer, you realized that it was the rocky part that you wanted. That is all part of the abductive process, and it is how designers think.

Other Applied Examples of Design Thinking

There are some other applied examples of design thinking worth a mention.

Wicked Problems: These are problems that have no apparent solution, no timeline for a solution, and no obvious path to a solution. Churchman described a seminar by Horst Rittel, who suggested:

"the term 'wicked problem' refers to that class of social system problems which are ill-formulated, where the information is confusing, where there are many clients and decision-makers with conflicting values, and where the ramifications in the whole system are thoroughly confusing. The adjective 'wicked' is supposed to describe the mischievous and even evil quality of these problems, where proposed 'solutions' often turn out to be worse than the symptoms."[28]

That sounds a lot like our complex conflicts, and the scientific literature on the topic recommends step-wise solutions very similar to what we're talking about.

Q Methodology: A similar approach was taken by Asah, et al.,[29] who were able to intervene in a live land-use conflict by applying Q methodology, in which you get participants to actively engage with the perspectives and frames of competing participants. These authors determined that simply by applying the research method, the participants changed their own frames just by actively engaging with the perspectives of opposing participants in a low-risk environment. That conflict was resolved as the participants reframed their positions and found enough common ground to base a mutually workable solution.

Defeasible Reasoning: Lawyers may be more like designers than you'd think. There is a type of reasoning that lawyers use that is very similar to abductive reasoning, called defeasible reasoning. It makes sense that lawyers would need something like this because they often operate in an environment where a decision needs to be made in the present, although the future is uncertain. When using defeasible reasoning, lawyers advocate for decisions which they openly admit are contingent on what they know now. For example, "Until fact XYZ is disproven, you have no choice but to decide in favor of my client." Abductive reasoning makes decisions that everyone acknowledges to be just one possible solution of many. There are a number of interesting resources on this topic, and I will not belabor the issue here. If you would like to go deeper on this topic, I've added some suggestions for further reading in the References section at the end of the book.[30]

Wrap-Up and What's Next

That was a lot to take in, so here's a quick summary.

- NDS gives us an overall context for why conflicts become complex and the importance of focusing effort on patterns of interaction between participants.

- The GMCR helps us focus on the participants who actually matter.
- Design Thinking helps us create those new patterns.

The next chapter section will summarize the seven important concepts to take away from what the science of complex conflicts tells us.

What Nature Teaches Us

We talked about sensemaking, nonlinear dynamical systems (NDS), the Graph Model for Conflict Resolution, and design thinking. That's a lot to take in, and it will be helpful at this point to summarize what all that means for our purposes. There are seven concepts that are going to help us overcome the Coherence Trap, get to the mindset of ROR, and show strategic leadership. These, by the way, are the seven principles of Focal Thinking.

1. Don't Control

The first thing that the science tells us is, don't try to control what can't be controlled. We get ourselves into trouble when we try to control the uncontrollable; to grasp at what cannot be held; to grip vapor. When we try to over-control a complex conflict, it is as if we are a young child running in the field under that murmuration of starlings, waving a butterfly net to catch them all at once. Our attempts are ineffective at best, potentially deadly at worst if the conflict is a violent one. Complex conflicts can't be controlled; they can only be influenced.

2. Don't Oversimplify

Don't oversimplify matters related to a complex conflict. We talked about frames and stereotypes and tricks that our mind plays on us to try to get us into the Coherence Trap so that we can feel comfortable, and that is exactly what we cannot afford to do. Oversimplification leads to missing the kind of nuances we will need in order to find resolution. If you have a favorite "-ism" that helps you make sense of the world, you'll need to be careful because you might be missing some important details that don't fit that approach. Concepts like colonialism, racism, capitalism, sexism, communism—and any other "-ism"—can be useful tools to help make sense of what you see around you, but the fewer you have in your analysis toolkit, the more you run the risk of oversimplifying matters. Focal Thinkers resist that urge at all costs.

66

3. Interactions Over Outcomes

In our approach to complex conflicts, we need to focus on interactions versus outcomes. We can't control the conflict, but we can influence where things go, and we do that by focusing on the patterns of interaction between the people involved. For example, if we know that our starlings only focus on the other birds in their direct proximity, that gives us something to work with. If we wanted to change the behavior of the entire murmuration, we might want to start by changing what each individual bird pays attention to. Imagine for a moment how the murmuration might change behavior if each starling focused not just on the birds one layer deep, but two or three layers deep. We might expect to see less volatility in the overall murmuration because the individuals would be focusing on a larger group by which they calibrate their own motion.

On the other hand, that pattern of interaction might make the flock less volatile, but when it did move, the movements would be more extreme and less finely-tuned since the birds would be moving in larger groups. Either way, we can only hope to change the behavior of a complex system like this by focusing on the patterns of interaction of those involved, but when we do, we can't immediately predict what's going to happen. This also happens to be a great way to help us release ourselves from responsibility for the outcome and step back a little bit and get some perspective, which is critical to making sure we don't oversimplify things and fall into the Coherence Trap.

4. Nudges Over Home Runs

When we start looking at interactions versus outcomes, it also helps to prioritize nudges over home runs. When we create strategies to solve a complex conflict, often, we try and solve the whole thing at once. That's our nature. And that is nothing more than us trying to assert control where we don't belong. If we can't control the outcome, we're not going to always get home runs. Furthermore, trying for a home run every time is going to be counterproductive because while we're swinging for the fences, we're inevitably going to miss some smaller opportunities that may have a bigger impact than we can predict. Remember, these systems are nonlinear, which means small things can have a big impact, and vice versa. The system can change dramatically with the smallest stimulus if they're in the right place at the right time. It's not about big wins; it's about small nudges in the right direction.

This is also important because sometimes an effective nudge won't even look like a win at first. For example, in one case that I worked on, we were able to nudge two people to connect with each other. One was in favor of the project, and the other was very much not. They had a mutual interest that enabled us to get them together in the same room, which itself was a bit of a small miracle. Just having them in the room together and connecting over common interest ended up changing the pattern of interaction between them in a very small, but what ended up being a very significant way. That meeting was not a home run. In fact, many on the team said it was a pointless idea because it wasn't going to accomplish anything, given their extreme difference of opinion. The team was trying to hit a home run when they could have been focused on nudging things in the right direction. Remember, the point here is to change the patterns of interaction and not focus necessarily on the outcomes.

5. More Complexity

It may sound counterintuitive, but what we're doing by nudging things in the right direction is trying to introduce more complexity into the system. How can that be, when things are already complex enough? Keep in mind that the end result of the Coherence Trap is patterns of dried-up interaction from oversimplification and blinders. If we're going to breathe new life into those interactions and get people to remove their blinders (or politely remove them on their behalf), the science tells us we want to focus on reintroducing the right kind of complexity to combat the oversimplification. We want to reintroduce a robust level of interaction into the system when we focus on the relationships between the parties and their patterns of interaction. This means doing things that disrupt the status quo and transform the dynamics between people in a system that has become over-simplified. We'll talk more about how to do this in the next section.

6. Power Versus Influence

The other very important aspect is power versus influence. Later we will discuss the fact that power is contextual to a specific decisive moment in the conflict. If someone can create a material change at a specific point in time, they have power. But when that important moment has passed, that may lose their power status.

Thinking back to the Graph Model for Conflict Resolution, I mentioned the fact that the model quickly bogged down if there were too many participants involved. This is like real life. Too many inputs make it impossible to really pay attention to all the possible outcomes. I discovered that to focus on the right participants, I had to look at their decision-making opportunities. Not everybody had the power in a conflict, so not everybody merited the same level of scrutiny. In other words, if you look for the people that can make the problem go away right now, that's where you focus first. Even if they're not on your side. *Especially* if they're not on your side.

There will be a few people in any conflict that are the core of the issue. Those are the people you need to focus on if they have the power to make the conflict end or change in a material way. And it always, always, always comes down to individuals, not companies or organizations. Focusing on organizations rather than people is just another set of blinders that won't really help. People make the decisions, so we need to focus on the people involved. You may not get to them directly, as we'll discuss later, but those are the ones that are at the heart of the issue.

For example, a regulatory body may have an incredible amount of power over an electric line transmission project, and you might want to focus your attention there. However, by doing that, you might miss the fact that the entire complaint being raised against the project is the result of one landowner who is being financially supported and encouraged by an environmental group to push the issue forward. If you can find a way to mitigate the influence of that environmental group on the individuals involved, suddenly, the contentious nature of the regulatory process changes. Similarly, a land-use battle may be brewing with a state or provincial government, and the governor is taking a challenging stance. That may boil down to the fact that she is beholden to a very small group that was key in getting her elected in the first place, and if you can get her enough wins to mitigate the support, you might be able to soften her position. Focusing on where the power lies enables us to bring some clarity to the situation, and then you can build strategies around that.

7. Resilience Over Consistency

The science also shows us that resilience is more important than consistency because we're dealing with dynamic, ever-changing systems. Many times, we will gather in groups and come up with strategies, and then the natural inclination is to stick with the strategy. That's just another example of trying to apply linear thinking to a curvy world. Remember, complex conflicts are inherently dynamic, so as soon as you have a strategy, it's pretty much guaranteed to be wrong tomorrow. If you're not constantly paying attention, you run the risk of missing the next nudge opportunity. Our natural need for coherence wants us to be consistent in our strategic approach, but that's not the right approach to a moving target that refuses to hold still. As we look at what nature teaches us, we learn that it's more important to be adaptable and resilient than it is to be consistent.

Wrap-Up and What's Next

Now you should have a better understanding of how some of the science on complex conflicts can help us understand complex conflicts and how to avoid the dreaded Coherence Trap in yourself and others. These approaches will provide the foundation for your ability to provide strategic leadership in complex conflicts by helping you know what to do next, and why to do it. Science might teach us a lot of valuable things about how nature works, but we're still going to have to deal with human nature, including our own. There are very good reasons why simply understanding complex conflicts as natural phenomena is not going to be enough to help us accomplish our objective here. Conflicts exist for a reason, and just knowing about birds and fish isn't going to get us where we need to go. We're going to need to take a minute to get honest with ourselves and take a good hard look at what we, as individuals and teams, need to be aware of before we can start putting all this to use.

Next, we'll have a look at the ways that our human nature creates obstacles to taking the advice of science so that we can eventually make a plan to get around that obstacle.

Human Nature is the Obstacle

We talked about the fact that nature is a great teacher. It can show us the way to make sense of complex conflicts because they behave very much like other complex natural systems. What we've learned so far are the seven principles of Focal Thinking:

1. Don't try to control things that can't be controlled
2. Don't oversimplify things just to feel comfortable
3. Focus on interactions, not outcomes
4. Aim for nudges, not home runs
5. Reintroduce the right kind of complexity back into the system
6. Pay attention to where the actual power lies
7. Prioritize resilience over consistency

But wait a minute, we're not entirely out of the woods yet. Just because something is natural doesn't mean it's good for you. As my grandmother used to say, "Nature ain't always your buddy." All those things might work in nature, but they tend to go against our *human nature,* and we're going to run the risk of getting in our own way if we're not careful. That's true with ourselves, conflict participants, and the teams with whom we work. In this section, we're going to point out some of the pitfalls that we're going to need to keep in mind as we start putting this all together.

As you might expect, our human nature is going to try to get in the way of implementing our approach to complex conflicts. And so is everyone else's, for that matter. If it were this easy, everyone would be already doing it. Here's why.

Against the Need for Coherence

We talked about the Coherence Trap and how we are hardwired to look for coherence from any possible source, even if we have to oversimplify things. We still have to overcome this, in ourselves and others, and that's an essential aspect of why nature's approach can be very difficult. We are going to have to deal with the fact that we won't always understand everything that's happening. That is the inherent nature of this type of undertaking, and it will never go away. That is very uncomfortable for us, and we need to, at all stages, grapple with that natural need for coherence. That's true for ourselves, our teams, and the people we're going to be trying to persuade.

Uncomfortable with Complexity

Another reason why this approach is going to be challenging for us is that it requires us to be comfortable with complexity. We talked about the fact that we won't necessarily make sense of it all, which means that we need to be comfortable with complex situations. That is not natural. That goes against our evolution, which tells us that uncertainty means risk, and risk means potential danger. Normal people try to avoid complexity at all costs. This is especially true of large projects, where our livelihoods and values are on the line. Depending on the folks you work for, admitting that you're not going to ever fully grasp how a conflict will unfold might also get in the way of your career. We obviously want to know the timeframe to be able to arrange the proper types of financing and do the necessary planning. Uncertainty around the timing and the outcome means it's more expensive. That is not only uncomfortable for us, but it also makes it very difficult to take the approach we're talking about because it calls out the fact that we can't know what's going to happen. But the finance people want us to know, or at least pretend that we know. That's part of their world, and it's also the world of the engineers and the folks that make stuff. Unfortunately, it's not the world of reality when it comes to complex conflicts. Dealing with the reality of uncertainty is not something that everyone in an organization involved in a large project is going to be comfortable with, for understandable reasons. However, the fact that uncertainty does not fit within a financial model or engineering diagram doesn't magically make it more certain. That is a cold hard reality of dealing with a complex situation like we're talking about, and we have the science to prove it.

High Degree of Collaboration

Another aspect of why our human nature is an obstacle is that this approach requires collaboration. Some organizations, especially large organizations, might not always be collaborative in nature. The approach we're talking about demands it, and that might not fit with your organization's culture. Even if they are collaborative within certain groups, they may or may not be collaborative across divisional silos or larger subsections of the company. The engineers might work well together, but perhaps not so much with the engagement teams or issues management folks. It's not enough for one group to be collaborative internally and then have other groups not be collaborative with them. That defeats the purpose, and it makes it virtually impossible to respond to the dynamic nature of a complex conflict. If we can't all respond on a collaborative basis, then our organizations can't bring the full breadth of their capabilities and expertise to bear in addressing and resiliently adapting to the problem. Our Apollo 13 team had lots of different disciplines working together, and that's what it takes.

Discomfort with Humility

Another reason why this is a challenge for people is the importance of humility. Collaboration will only get you so far without a sense of humility to go with it. When I went to business school and law school, they didn't have Humility Training 101 anywhere in the curriculum. It wasn't part of any syllabus I ever saw in college. Humility is not a value generally appreciated in our world, and especially not among hard-driving people who accomplish things at the scale that we're talking about. Humility is taken as weakness, and weakness is a virtual guarantee that one's career will not advance. The problem with this sad reality is that it gets in the way of the kind of agile responsiveness your organization will need to remain resilient in the face of complexity. An organization cannot be resilient in the face of change if its people don't have the humility to adapt in a team context.

Specifically, this means if someone on the team comes up with an idea or a strategy, then that person needs to be humble enough to jettison it the instant something better comes along. Otherwise, you run the real danger of being consistent when you ought to be resilient. This is tough for people to take, especially if they work in an organization in which people don't have the psychological safety to allow them to try new things. But if we're going to stay resilient in the face of change, we need to prioritize the idea over the person that came up with it. Ideas can come from anywhere regardless of that person's place on the hierarchy of the organization. An organization that has hierarchical constraints essentially puts a lid on its own growth potential. This is not down to the team members themselves; it's a function of leadership. A good leader can create an environment that values ideas over their source and make sure people are comfortable being humble enough to give up their pet idea.

Undervaluing Persuasion

The next element of why nature is a bit of an obstacle for us is that this approach requires us to be comfortable with persuasion. The key to persuading someone to do something is to give them something first. As the saying goes, you need to give to get. When you're dealing with a conflict, however, this can be difficult. It's a tough sell to be able to say to an organization that the detractors need to get something from you if you want them to give you what you want to. Remember that in a conflict, it's often more about lose-lose than win-win. This can be counterintuitive. However, it is the only way that you will get people to change their behavior. So, this approach is challenging for people because it forces them to look at the motivations and the behavior drivers of others and use that motivation to get people to do what they want them to do. A conflict is not the natural place for someone to look at how to serve others with what they need but is it is exactly what needs to happen in order to change the patterns of interaction.

Ryan Holiday describes how John F. Kennedy's rose to the challenge of the Cuban missile crisis, noting how influential this passage from strategist B. H. Liddell Hart was on Kennedy's success:

> "Have unlimited patience. Never corner an opponent, and always assist him to save face. Put yourself in his shoes—so as to see things through his eyes. Avoid self-righteousness like the devil—nothing is so self-blinding."[31]

This can be a tough one for people to wrap their minds around. It also needs to be said, putting it bluntly, that large projects haven't traditionally required marketing or persuasive communications, but that's starting to bite them in the behind now. Consumer packaged goods (CPG) companies are geniuses at this because they have to be— it's life or death for their highly-competitive business.

74

Large projects have never really needed that level of expertise at the organizational level, and so that muscle has never been developed. PR, yes. Engagement, yes. Community Relations, yes. But not necessarily marketing communications or branding. And guess what? Those days are over. Companies that are trying to accomplish things at a large scale need to start paying attention to the human landscape and how to be truly, enduringly persuasive at all levels. It may be time to take a few lessons from the CPG folks and pump that persuasion muscle because just shouting facts and statistics isn't going to help the cause. If you can't find a way to connect emotionally with the folks you're impacting, you're going to miss some critical opportunities to make things happen.

Undervaluing Nudges

The last one is something we've briefly touched on before, and that's the idea of nudges over home runs. When we feel we need to get a big win, that's mostly us saying we need to be in control. But we're not in control. We never will be in control. We can't be in control. And we shouldn't try to be in control. A home run is not something necessarily to look for. But a nudge is. A nudge is us exerting influence over a pattern of interaction. It's not the same as a big win because it may not look like a win when we do it. Like I talked about before, if you get two opposing people in a room together, even if it's full of other people, over some shared interest, that can be a nudge in the right direction. No one would call that a win, but it may lead to a win. The difference is important when dealing with your teams because if everyone is trying to hit a home run and look like the hero, then everybody will be swinging for the fences, and people will miss relevant opportunities right in front of them. They will also falsely reject an opportunity that might be useful. If they're looking for wins as opposed to nudges, they will miss the small patterns of interaction change that can be incredibly useful. This is how we cross that rive one stone at a time, using our abductive reasoning skills to become design thinkers.

Wrap-Up and What's Next

Now that we know the ways human nature—ours, and that of all the other conflict participants—might get in the way of taking the steps we need to take to show strategic leadership, we can put together a plan to deal with that obstacle.

Next, we will talk about the path to overcoming that obstacle—by heading right at it.

SECTION FOUR: PUTTING IT TO WORK

A t the beginning of this book, I mentioned that this was going to be a journey of self-discovery because it's our thinking that needs to change if we're going to show strategic leadership in complex conflicts. As it turns out, the path to making sense of it all lies primarily in managing our own ability to overcome the obstacles that our human nature creates for ourselves and our teams. The philosopher Marcus Aurelius said, "The impediment to action advances action. What stands in the way becomes the way." In other words, the obstacle in front of us is precisely the path that we should take. Don't run from it, face it directly, and tackle it head-on. Since nature is both our teacher and our obstacle, it's going to be helpful to think of that obstacle as the path forward. The task now is to make sure that the obstacles our human nature puts in front of us are addressed directly as we try to make sense of complexity.

It's one thing to achieve stillness, Zen or ROR within yourself, but quite another to do so in your team, another to do it for your company, and yet another to do so with your detractors. Nevertheless, that's your mandate. As we've discussed, the key is to not to be outcome-focused but process-focused. Learning to trust the process and let go of the outcome that neither you, nor anyone can guarantee in the first place.

In this section, we are going to lay out a path that you can follow to make this happen. This is all based on the science we just learned, the obstacles our human nature puts in front of us, and the professional experience of myself and those I admire. My goal is for this to be a checklist you can use to create your own path through the complexity of whatever conflict you may face along the way.

Here's an overview of the main points:

1. Create a Human Landscape Model
2. Shake Up the Interactions
3. Be Persuasive in the Office
4. Stay Resilient

Create a Human Landscape Model

The first step along the path to getting to that point of Release, Observe and Revisit so we can avoid the Coherence Trap is to create a model of the human landscape in our particular situation. This will give us a complete, holistic, comprehensive picture of the situation. As my engineering colleagues like to call it, this is a model of the "non-technical requirements." Just like our Apollo 13 engineers needed to have all the available pieces of the puzzle spread out on the table, you can't design a solution to something unless you see all the moving parts at once. Even if you do nothing else, this part of the process is incredibly valuable because it gives you a birds-eye view of everyone involved in the conflict. That alone is worth the effort, just so you have a sense of comfort knowing that you have access to the full list of everybody involved. See? Just imagining that brought your stress levels down a bit, didn't it?

Organize by the Key Moments

A very effective way to keep track of hundreds of conflict participants without oversimplifying matters is to focus on the inflection points in the conflict. Think of these as Key Moments that might make a material change to the conflict. When our flock of starlings makes a sudden and dramatic shift in direction, some event triggered them, and that is a great place to focus our efforts. In our conflicts, we won't always be able to foresee all these Key Moments, but there will be some that we can predict or that are baked into the conflict. By filtering all the information coming at us in context of these moments, we will be able to organize our thinking strategically and still be able to put all the various players involved in context without relegating them to a convenient but inaccurate frame.

Key Moments can be formal project milestones that we know well in advance, such as city council sessions, regulatory approval meetings, and Tribal votes. When we know these types of inflection points, we can plan around that specific event and focus our efforts to make sure it goes the way we want it to. Earlier, we talked about distinguishing power versus influence. *Power is contextual.* Different Key Moments will have different power individuals. A city councilor may have the power to make a material change in a conflict up to the point of a council vote, but afterward, they may be only influential. Or possibly irrelevant.

Key Moments can also be less structured conversations that will likely happen sometime in the future. For example, in a presidential transition, the time between the election and inauguration is a busy time of policy-making. If your project is going to come up in those discussions, you will want to plan in advance for when that discussion happens to make sure it goes your way. It might not be formally scheduled, but if you know it's going to happen at some point, then you need to get ready for it.

Key Moments can also be completely unforeseen. In fact, most of them will be. That's the unknowable nature of probabilistic complexity. Stuff just happens. This fact will heighten the importance of our team to be resilient and your organization to be adaptable in the face of the inevitable dynamic change. When the only certainty is uncertainty, paying attention to Key Moments along the way provides a solid foundation for our ability to adapt in the moment.

If you find yourself getting overwhelmed (and you will), go back to the Key Moments that create inflection points in the conflict and start from there.

Background Research

Another useful step in getting a handle on the human landscape is to do some research. I like to do a combination of secondary and primary research, and I'll show you some easy ways to do it even if you don't have a research background.

To do the secondary (i.e. indirect) research, I start by reading everything I can get my hands on related to the conflict and the people involved. This includes news articles, academic articles, regulatory rulings, legal cases, internal client documents, videos, audio recordings—anything and everything that will relate to the conflict. This allows me to get a sense of what's going on and who is involved. Within a very short time, you're going to start feeling that discomfort that comes from overwhelming complexity, as your linear-thinking mind starts to panic with all the information you're taking in. You're going to start second-guessing yourself and your ability to make any sense of it. You may also start cursing my name and ruing the day you bought this book. And you'll definitely wish you hadn't bought 20 copies to give to your friends and colleagues. A great way to keep your head above water is to avoid reading passively. Organize the information as you go. Otherwise, you're going to get bogged down in the minutiae pretty quickly.

You'll want to keep track of four things as you read:

1. Participants (individuals & organization)
2. Themes that emerge
3. Quotes worth keeping
4. The relevant Key Moments

As you wade through the mountains of information, organizing it all this way will make it easier to access it when the later stages of the analysis happen, and it will keep you from panicking and falling into the Coherence Trap. You can use a big sheet of oversized paper to do this, but it's going to get unwieldy pretty quickly. I've used spreadsheets before, but with the mountain of information you'll be taking in, it's not always practical. The other problem with spreadsheets is that you can't see the big picture at once.

I like to use software programs designed for qualitative data analysis. There are a few good ones out there, but I tend to gravitate to ones that have drag-and-drop functionality that makes it easy to create nodes of information visually. The workspace ends up looking like a few dozen multicolored circles, each of which represents content that I drag-and-drop into it. I organize the nodes by participants and themes, and each node contains relevant background information. Be sure to pick something easy and intuitive without a big learning curve. There are also stakeholder management platforms that can help, but they're not as visual as you might need at this early stage. They are great tools once you get rolling, but you need something unstructured and visual to get things started.

When I look for themes, I try to pay attention to issues that keep coming up over and over again. For example, in one conflict I was helping with, the issue of land-use was complicated by the level of Indigenous land ownership, and that carried a whole series of other challenges: colonialism, racism, sexism, violence, self-governance, conflict of laws, and others. Keeping track of those themes will help you make sense of the various aspects of the conflict so that you can bring some sense of order to it later. Your Human Landscape Model should also keep track of all the people involved, including individuals and the organizations associated with them. As we mentioned previously, most complex conflicts revolve around specific individuals, so it's essential to have a sense of who's who. The value in using a qualitative data analysis program is that it will also enable you to pull out quotes that represent the themes and ideas you're finding as you go. That's very important when it comes time to report back to the team, or when you've been working on the conflict for months and want to find something a key player said earlier.

As you do this, be sure to make note of the formal and informal known Key Moments. When it comes to distinguishing, who has power and who only has influence, the context of the triggering event will be extremely helpful down the road.

Primary Research

The next stage is to consider doing primary research, i.e. hearing it directly from the people involved. Doing the secondary research first is a great way to get a sense of who's involved and what themes come up, but there's no substitute for getting straight from the source. That firsthand knowledge will help fill many of the knowledge gaps that the secondary documents can't or won't cover. It will also help you get updated, timely information because by the time it gets written down, the information is very likely to be stale, given the dynamic nature of the conflicts you'll be dealing with. I always like to say that insight delayed is insight denied. When time is a factor, you'll want to place a premium on the folks who can get you the direct information in real-time.

When you're deciding whom to contact, here are some things to consider. Look for people who are directly involved in some part of the conflict. This can be engagement team members, protesters, adjudicators, proponents, issues management staff, landowners, and so forth. You want people who are directly impacted, either by virtue of their jobs, their passions, or their (un)willing participation. Whenever you do research like this, you only want to ask people things about which they have some expertise, and that usually means some direct involvement. Another group to look for is people who have informed opinions. This can include legal counsel, executives, reporters, academics, or other people who have a reason to pay attention and are knowledgeable, but may not be directly in the day-to-day of the conflict. These folks can offer valuable perspectives that will help you paint the larger picture.

One important thing to keep in mind throughout the process is that at this point, you don't care what side of the conflict they are on, and they don't need to be objective about their opinion. Often I will quote content or individuals who are very clearly antagonistic to my client's perspective. I sometimes need to remind them that we're not dealing with objective truth here; we're dealing with the *perceptions* of incompatible activity. If something exists in someone's mind, that's going to influence their behavior regardless of how true it might be. The more comprehensive the range of diversity you can find at the outset, the more useful your Human Landscape Model is going to be. What you don't want is to skip over any themes or perspectives that don't align with your own biases. That leads to the Coherence Trap, which will put a quick end to your sensemaking activity. More information is better, and the more contradictory the perspectives and themes you come up with, the more trustworthy your analysis is going to be. Get all those pieces out on the table now, just like the Apollo 13 engineers, because you're going to need them soon.

Categorize the Participants

The next level of the Human Landscape Model is to start categorizing people as being supporters, detractors, and neutrals. This enables you to get a sense of who will be in support of the project, who is going to get in the way, and who is a neutral third-party. It's important to remember that these will change often. One person might be a supporter today, but they may be a detractor tomorrow, so keep your wits about you.

I had a colleague who spent time in military intelligence, and I brought him in to speak with some clients about his experiences and approach to managing complex conflicts. When he was in Afghanistan, part of his role was to be among the first to go into new villages as part of the advance team. Their approach was not too far off what we're talking about here. They would quickly get a sense of which villagers were happy to have them around, which were going to wait and see, which were openly hostile, and which were quietly hostile. The happy-to-see you group was not their priority because, in an open conflict, they were not an immediate threat. The wait-and-see were usually the majority because that part of the world had seen foreign armies come and go for Millennia, and this was just another group passing through. The openly hostile people were more of a concern for obvious reasons, but not nearly as much as the quietly hostile ones. If someone was openly hostile, they were at least communicating something to them. In a sense, there was some dialogue happening. It was the folks that were quietly hostile that were the most dangerous because they had shut down all intention of communication. They had reached the point of dried-up engagement. They were very likely to do something violent or work with those in the region willing to do something violent on their behalf.

One of the biggest challenges was to tell the difference between the wait-and-see folks and the quietly hostile ones. Once they were able to categorize the people, they engaged with them accordingly. The happy-to-see-you and wait-and-see people were given every opportunity to profit from the presence of the troops in a way that was appropriate and consistent with the village culture. The openly hostile people were given the same opportunities to win them over, although they usually needed extra attention, and they tended to stay clear. The quietly hostile ones got most of the attention and were watched very, very carefully.

Hopefully, the conflicts you're going to be dealing with won't involve life and death to this degree, although they obviously might. In either case, the categorization process is the same. You need to be clear where everyone stands and be ready to change them up when they switch their perspective. In the software you use, you'll want to have a way to flag their status so you can easily categorize them.

Identify the Likely Next Step

The GMCR methodology that I used to model the conflict in my original research was based on the idea that you want to pay attention to the next likely decision a participant is going to want to make. That taught me the importance of focusing on what they're likely to do next, as well as helping me winnow the focus to the folks with power. It's always helpful to understand people's motivations, but we're more focused on action and the expression of power. The truly interesting nugget is to start looking for what is their next decision likely to be. That way, you can focus more on their actions than their motivations and be ready to influence those actions when the opportunity comes. What you'll find is that motivations are more long-term, and the next decisions are more in the moment. When we're dealing with a dynamic system, guess which one is more useful.

Here's a quick example of the difference between motivation and a next decision. In a recent conflict, a very senior elected official owed her election to three local regions. Her electoral mandate was relatively thin, so she was very motivated to keep those three regions happy. Those regions were remote and rural, and they happened to be very focused on environmental issues. That fact influenced her approach to the conflict at hand, which would express itself at any given point in time. At one point, when it came time to make a decision around how she was going to approach land use consultation with Indigenous groups, she had a decision to make around the peripheral groups that would be part of the engagement process: how much would the environmental NGOs play a role, and be seen to be playing a role, so that she could reinforce her environmental *bona fides* with her power base? As decision times continually came up, that motivation drove her next choice, but when we're working with a constantly changing dynamic system, we're much more interested in what's coming at us right now. That's best expressed in terms of the next decision the participants are likely to make. Focusing on the next likely decision forces us to get into the mindset of the people we're dealing with and brings us into a more practical realm.

Distinguish Power from Influence

One of the most important aspects of making sense of complexity is knowing what to filter out. Complex conflicts are challenging because we generally have no decision-making guidelines about what to filter out when we're overloaded. That is why, in our natural need for coherence, we make up our own guidelines about what we will pay attention to and what we will ignore. According to our model of how conflicts happen, oversimplification of reality leads to a general breakdown of patterns of communication between conflict participants. Not only does this create conflicts in the first place, but it also contributes to their longevity. When we filter out the wrong information, it doesn't serve us well.

We're all smart, so you're never going to solve a conflict by being smarter than everyone else. With Focal Thinking, the point isn't how much you know; it's about knowing where to focus. We have to get that part right first. Recall our Apollo 13 design thinking example. The engineers in Houston needed to have access to all the components available on the spaceship as they were designing the makeshift CO_2 scrubber. If they had been missing key elements, it would have been impossible to synthesize something that worked. In the same way, if they had too many useless materials to work with, they might have been overwhelmed into inaction. Knowing what to filter is critical to the entire process. If we get it right at the start, we will be able to know which of the many incoming stimuli we should focus on, and which we should set aside for later.

Back when I was doing my doctoral research using the GMCR, I got to the heart of the conflict by finding the groups who were directly at odds. They were 180 degrees opposed to each other, and there was no apparent opportunity for alignment. I discarded those that were mostly opposed, but not necessarily 180 degrees in opposition. Some of the others I temporarily removed were only influencing the groups that were opposed. I quickly realized that the model worked when I was clear on the groups that were in total head-to-head opposition with each other. Once I found them, the possible future states went down to a manageable number, and it was easy to find the current and desired states from that group.

What worked for the model also works in reality. When we can focus on where the real conflict lies, in the midst of all the various influencers and co-participants, it is much easier to focus on the things that matter. We don't have to oversimplify; we have to focus on the difference between power and influence.

Participants with power are those who can make an immediate, direct, and material change to the conflict. In our case, that is the point when a conflict system changes direction. If we go back to our murmuration of starlings example, it would be that moment when the group suddenly changes shape or direction, and the same idea holds true for a conflict system. I like to start with the people who have the power to make the conflict go away entirely because that is a great way to make sure your strategic recommendations are going to have maximum impact and focus. When you're trying to explain what to do next and why to do it, focusing on the real power is a great place to start. The point is not to get them to stop the conflict, but to make sure your plans are pointed in the right direction and you know what to filter out when new information comes at you. Let's refer to the folks who can make an immediate and material impact on the conflict system as *Conflict Drivers*. There are also going to be people who do not have the power to make an immediate, material impact, but can influence those who can do so. Let's call them *Conflict Influencers*.

Focusing on the immediacy of the impact, for Drivers and Influencers, is a necessary by-product of the fact that these conflicts are dynamic. Since they're always changing, we are forced to pay attention to the issues in front of us right now. If they were static, we could wax eloquent about all the possible Influencers and Drivers and make long-term plans and strategies. But we don't have that luxury in a dynamic environment. We need to deal with what we have today.

You will notice the overlap with Key Moments and Conflict Drivers. If you look at your conflict by Key Moments, you'll want to include an analysis of the Conflict Drivers who will be (or were) part of making that moment happen. Similarly, if you're focusing more on the Conflict Drivers, keep an eye out for the Key Moments when they're likely to exert their power. These are two sides to the same coin, so don't ignore one for the other. No power, no Key Moments. No Key Moments, no power.

Example: Northern Gateway

My research on the Northern Gateway project will be a target-rich environment for examples, because it was very complex. I am not going to belabor the details, but here are the main elements to give you some context. At the time of the project, Canadian oil traded at a discount compared to the Brent benchmark because of its remote nature, the costs of transportation, and dependence on the US market for all sales. In 2014 alone, this cost the people of Canada $7.3 billion in lost potential tax revenue.[32] The Northern Gateway pipeline route would have been 1,170 kilometers from the prairies of Bruderheim, Alberta to the coastal tidewater of Kitimat, British Columbia.

There were five primary challenges to the project. First, the pipeline was linked to opposition to the Alberta oil sands, the source of the pipeline contents.[33] While the pipelines may be the most efficient and comparatively least risky of the other transportation alternatives, they remain tied to the concerns around the production source, a contributor to global greenhouse gas emissions (GHG). Second, Northern Gateway was a so-called greenfield project, meaning that it would go through land currently undeveloped for such infrastructure. Third, the indigenous land claim situation in Canada is generally unsettled, particularly in the province of British Columbia, so any project that proposes to cross those territories would have additional complexities. Not only are many land claims not settled, but there were dozens of Indigenous bands along the proposed route, each of which has the potential power to stop or hinder the approval process.[34]

Fourth, the project would cross countless rivers and streams, giving cause for concern over the ecological impacts of the project itself as well as any potential spill. Fifth, the Douglas Channel to Kitimat is approximately 90 nautical miles long and relatively narrow at between 1 to 3.5 nautical miles wide, raising concerns about marine shipping safety. The shadow of the Exxon Valdez spill and a more recent grounding of the British Columbia Ferries ship *Queen of the North* loomed large in the public's mind.

Conflict Influencers

We will start our discussion off with Conflict Influencers. A good example might be environmental non-governmental organizations (ENGOs). When I was researching the Northern Gateway conflict, I was repeatedly told that ENGOs were important Conflict Drivers and that I had to include them in the overall analysis. Fair enough. But as I started adding them to the GMCR model, I started noticing that they did not have any appreciable impact on the various future states the model created, other than the fact that they clogged it up with hundreds of potential future outcomes that weren't that helpful to the analysis.

What I quickly realized was that ENGOs were influential, but they were not Conflict Drivers because they couldn't make the conflict go away right now. Or ever, for that matter. At certain points in time, they could bring litigation and take steps to influence the outcome of the process, but that is all they are doing—influencing. This is primarily why ENGOs align with Conflict Drivers who are closer to the decision-making core. For example, many ENGOs will align with Indigenous groups with whom they can make common cause. In the Northern Gateway example, many ENGOs persuasively used arguments related to the very legitimate issues of Indigenous sovereignty, oppression, and colonization, and effectively used those to generate support against the project.

Another illustrative example of a Conflict Influencer from my research on Northern Gateway is the producers—the oil company customers who would've been purchasing capacity in the pipelines to ship their product. Almost everyone that was part of my research indicated that the producers were a key decision-maker in the conflict because if they chose not to sign advanced contracts before a certain stage of project completion, the project would not meet conditions set out by the energy regulator. The producers' decisions would indeed impact the outcome of the project. However, they were not Conflict Drivers until the moment came for them to decide to sign the agreements to ship. Until that time, they are not Drivers because they would not have had the power to stop the conflict or change it materially. Until it is time for you to have a material impact, you are not a Driver. You can be influential, certainly. You can also be the target of influence based on your future status as a possible Driver. But you are not one *right now*. In a dynamic system, if you're not powerful today, you're not powerful at all.

Another example of a Conflict Influencer from Northern Gateway was the regulatory body. At the time of my research, the regulator had already conditionally approved the project, so while many thought it should be a Conflict Driver, it simply wasn't at that time; in that context. When it came time for them to determine if the 209 approval conditions had been met, their influence would have been immediate and material, but that was not the case when I was undertaking my analysis.

This is one of the hardest things to wrap your mind around, but it is vital that you do so. Remember that systems are based in time, and this is one of the ramifications of that fact. You need to resist the urge to include everyone at once and try to make sense of it all at once. That is tantamount to trying to catch the entire murmuration of starlings with one net. It is not possible. Don't try. Attempting to do that is part of what creates the Coherence Trap in the first place. Distinguishing Influencers from Drivers is one of the most important things you need to do differently, based on your new way of thinking.

Conflict Drivers

One example of a Conflict Driver in Northern Gateway was the federal government. At the time I conducted my research, the federal government was in a position to stop the project. At that time, the energy regulator had already conditionally approved the project, and the previous government had given their assent. However, the newly-elected government was publicly opposed to the project, and they had several passive ways to prevent it. In this case, there were many procedural opportunities for them to ensure not all the 209 conditions were met in time, and in fact, that's what they ended up doing. Because the tidewater port was at the end of a long, narrow channel, the federal government was able to formalize a previously informal moratorium on shipping in that general area, but only for ships carrying Alberta-sourced bitumen. Others got a pass. They could have easily gone either direction, but they chose to actively prevent ships in that area, although by international law, they could only block domestic shipping. In the model I created using the GMCR, this proved to be an example of a Conflict Driver because they had a direct, material impact on the state of the project at the time.

Wrap-Up and What's Next

When you're done with this first step of creating the Human Landscape Model, you will already have created a great deal of value. You will have collected all the relevant participants in one place, you'll know which ones are pro, anti, and neutral, you'll have a good understanding of their motivations and next likely actions, and you will know which ones are critical right now. More importantly, you now have a framework on which you can build your strategic planning, and which you can use to give context to the continually updated information that's going to be coming at you. The Human Landscape Model will be very helpful to our goal of knowing what to do next, and why. You will be coming back to this daily, keeping it updated, and referring to it as you build the strategic context for what to do next and why do it.

Fight Different

Next, we're going to talk about how to shake up the existing patterns of interaction so you can start reinvigorating those dried-up patterns that created and perpetuated the conflict in the first place.

Change the Interactions

"You don't convince people by challenging their longest and most firmly held opinions. You find common ground and work from there. Or you look for leverage to make them listen. Or you create an alternative with so much support from other people that the opposition voluntarily abandons its views and joins you camp."

Ryan Holiday, *The Obstacle is the Way*

The next stage in putting Focal Thinking to work is to look for ways to shake up the existing patterns of interaction. We talked about the fact that we're not focusing on outcomes first. We're looking at the interactions between people—especially the Conflict Drivers with power and the Conflict Influencers who can sway them. We want to find the small nudges that will reintroduce a healthy level of complexity to a system bogged down by previously dried-up patterns of interaction. This will be an important part of your ability to show strategic leadership because, after this, you'll be able to explain not only what to do next, but why to do it.

The most important aspect of any pattern shake-up tactic is the extent to which it will get participants to effectively engage with each other's perspectives. The more a tactic can encourage that to happen where it hadn't before, the more likely it will be to succeed. In addition to encouraging participants to get into each other's heads, effective tactics will also promote new patterns of interaction, directly or indirectly. Encouraging participants to see each other in a new light, in ways that break down their stereotypes or oversimplifications of each other can also help kick-start an environment where new patterns of interaction can take hold.

There are many ways to accomplish this, and this section will cover some useful considerations by which you can judge how likely a tactic is to succeed.

Decide on the Future State

The first step in shaking up the patterns of interaction is to get clear about the future state you want to create. "Stopping the conflict" is not a future state, by the way. It's more helpful if the future state is related to the Conflict Drivers; those who could stop the conflict or create an immediate, material change to the system.

In many cases, the ideal future state is going to be directly related to the formal or informal Key Moments that create inflection points in the conflict. If we know something is coming up that is going to have a material change to the conflict, whether we know exactly when it's coming or not, we can just decide that the ideal future state would be for that the Key Moment to go our way. On the other hand, the ideal future state might be a much larger goal as it relates to groups or individual patterns of interaction. The point here is that, in order to be strategic in our approach, we need to know precisely what we're aiming for.

We were recently working with an Indigenous group to get a project approved. Some were on our side, and some were not. The project had unearthed some pretty serious divisions within the band that had been simmering for decades, and we had stepped right in the middle of it. In this case, there were two main antagonists. If these individuals were able to choose somehow to work together and engage, the entire conflict would take a dramatic, material change. That's how we knew where to focus the effort towards our future state goal. What we needed to do was to get these two to find a measure of common ground that would change their dried-up patterns of interaction. Even if that meant simply getting them in a room together at the same time, not to engage or even talk, but simply to be in the same room. To this point, their interactions were virtually nil because they had fallen into a very deep Coherence Trap.

That's it. That's the extent of the future state we were hoping for. We weren't trying to get them to hold hands, set aside their issues, and greet the project with open arms and tears of gratitude. We just needed to get them in the same room at the same time. Would that solve the conflict? No. Would it get the project approved? No. Would it heal their divisions? No. Would it be a home run? Not even close. Would it shake up the current patterns of interaction? Yes. Would it nudge things in the right direction? Absolutely.

Here's where you can go back to your Human Landscape Model, find the Conflict Drivers, and start looking at the ideal future state that you need to achieve. There may be several that you have in mind, and that's fine. The point is, focus on the Conflict Drivers and dream of a way to change how they're interacting right now. That's your goal.

And yes, that goal will change. Many times. Probably tomorrow, as a matter of fact. That's all part of dealing with a dynamic system. Don't get too attached to that goal. Just get ready to start things moving right now with what you've got in front of you today.

Find the Persuasion Pinch Points

Once you have a clear idea of your ideal future state, no matter how simple or small it may appear, then you can start looking for the persuasion pinch points that will get in your way. These are areas where if we apply the proper amount of persuasion, we will be able to get people to interact with each other the way we want them to, and identifying them is critical.

Let's go back to our example of getting the two Conflict Drivers in the same room together. The challenge was pretty evident in that case. They pretty much hated each other, and both had strong reasons for it. They were also in the position of being de facto leaders of the two groups that were divided, which put extra pressure on them to maintain the current antagonistic state. Even if, at some point, they wanted to change how they interacted, it would jeopardize their leadership status. The persuasion pinch point, in this case, was how to find a way to get them in the same physical space at the same time that was so compelling they couldn't ignore it.

Create Coalitions

The next stage is to create coalitions around the Conflict Drivers. If two people are never going to change their conflict with each other, because it's rooted in deeply seated values or for whatever reason, then don't try to push that stone uphill. Focus instead on building coalitions of people around the power structure in a way that will help dislodge those current patterns of interaction. You may never get them to agree, but you might get them to change just enough to get the things done that you need to. Looking for those coalitions is an essential element of being able to get the conflict moving.

In this example, if we had phoned each of the Conflict Drivers and said, "Hey, do you folks want to get in the same room and hash this out? There are probably lots of ways we can start working together," we would've been dead in the water. However, if someone else suggested that idea, or if there was something they could do in common that their own groups would give them leeway to participate in despite all their differences, that might accomplish the immediate goal. In this case, we found that common element that neither side could afford to say no to. There was a senior government official who was very well regarded by this community, and the opportunity came up for us to arrange to have her speak. By inviting both Conflict Drivers to that event, we were able to get them in the same room together at the same time, along with their respective camps.

This is where things like cultural and civic events can be so powerful. There are reasons diplomats use cultural and sporting initiatives to lay the groundwork for future relationships. They offer something that everyone can agree upon and feel comfortable attending; a kind of neutral territory where competing factions can set aside differences for a moment. This is especially true in smaller communities and remote areas, where cultural events take on extra significance because they help validate the existence of the community in the first place. A local fun run or arts festival or concert may look like small potatoes to people living in urban centers, but these events are not just for entertainment; they also validate the community itself. Participation in these types of events, formally or informally, can a great way to build coalitions and reinvigorate positive patterns of interaction.

This step is very important, so I want to give an example of how it might apply at a macro level, not just for small groups of individuals. To do this, I'll introduce the idea of finding commonalities and threads.

Finding Commonalities and Threads

To build coalitions at a more macro level, think of commonalities and threads between the Conflict Drivers and Influencers. *Commonalities* will deal with reality and *threads* with the perception of reality. Recall our definition of conflict: relational processes influenced by the perception of incompatible activities. Let's think of commonalities as compatible activities that overlap between participants. Note that this does not include the perception of overlap. Two participants may have activities that are fully compatible, but they may not realize it, or they may not yet see it that way. For example, an energy regulator and an Indigenous group may both be interested in protecting the environment, even though they may see each other as having antagonistic objectives.

The perception side of the equation comes in to play with the threads we draw between the commonalities. In the preceding example, the thread we might draw between the common goal between an Indigenous group and the regulator might be to get everyone to understand and believe that the goals are the same even though their approach differs. That won't solve it, but it's a nudge in the right direction, and that's what we're looking for. Commonalities and threads are critical to the Focal Thinking process. A similar idea is represented in Coleman, et al.,[35] in which the authors remind us of the "the third side" concept from Fisher & Ury.[36] The idea here is to take advantage of parties not directly involved in the conflict, or at least not in full-blown opposition, to get leverage on those who are.

As you look for commonalities and threads between the participants, you can tackle them in any order. I found it helpful to focus on the Influencers first because their positions are easier to align, and there is less direct conflict between them. Once you get a handle on who the Influencers currently are, it will be easier to turn attention to the Conflict Drivers and how to persuade them. It is also helpful to address the participants by category because that will help provide a measure of structure to the process. It is easy to get caught up in the complexity of options and permutations involved, and any structure you can bring to the process will be helpful. The objective will be to create blocs of Influencers by identifying their overlapping interests. It might be helpful to think of it as a series of Venn diagrams where we build coalitions of mutual interest.

Influencer-to-Influencer Commonalities and Threads

The easiest part of this step is to find commonalities between Influencers and connect the threads. An example from my research that I just alluded to was the common cause that the energy regulator

95

had with the land-based Indigenous groups in protecting the environment. They did not disagree about its importance; some of them just disagreed on how it was to be accomplished. Had they been at Driver-level conflict, the regulator might have been actively seeking to despoil the environment purposefully. There are countries in which that is a reality. The perceptual thread between them was difficult to connect, however, because of ongoing concerns and disagreements about the process by which the conclusions were reached. In the end, the regulator agreed with the proponent's proposal but placed a total of 209 substantive conditions on the final approval. Regarding our Driver/Influencer analysis, these two participant groups were not in 180-degree opposition.

As we look for commonalities and threads, there are a few techniques that you can use. If you are a list maker, you might want to make a list of the coalitions on a spreadsheet or some sort of table with rows and columns. If you are more of a visual thinker, sketching them out on a large sheet of paper is a good way to organize your ideas. You can also use the qualitative data analysis software we talked about earlier. This is one way we will be putting abductive reasoning to work for us. The route will be a crooked line, and it will be impossible to tell what stones will get us to the other side until we venture out into the first one. We won't even know if there is a path that will get us there. All we know is that we need to get to the other side and that if we find the right stones along the way, we will be successful.

The important thing to remember is that the final result is not the goal of this part of the process; instead, it is the thinking along the way. You may sketch out dozens of different options and throw away a lot of paper. It is critical that you give yourself the freedom to do this. Many of us will try to get it right the first time by creating the ultimate visual or spreadsheet on the first attempt. Give yourself some freedom to experiment and play with it. For just a few minutes, take yourself back to your childhood and just put whatever comes to mind on paper. Nobody will grade it. Nobody will judge it. Nobody will censor it. Nobody will even see it. If your mind is not free to wander and explore at this stage, you are going to miss some interesting possibilities.

Change the Interactions

Influencer-to-Driver Commonalities and Threads

The next step in the process is to start finding alignment between the Conflict Influencers and Drivers. This will enable you to start looking at where the possible coalitions might be. This is much easier to do once you have identified blocs of Influencers with commonalities. For those who are visually oriented, here is a useful approach. Use a large piece of paper. Put each Key Moment into a shape (square, circle, etc.) on opposite extreme ends of the paper. This signifies the distance between their positions, but it will also give you space to put the coalitions of Influencers that will help bridge that divide. Now sketch out the Influencer coalitions you have already identified and put them in the middle area. Try the first configuration that makes sense to you and think about what it is that overlaps and where the commonalities lie. Try a few different ones, and see where your thinking takes you.

This sounds unstructured and nebulous because it is supposed to be that way at this stage. If this is vaguely uncomfortable, that is a sign that you are on the verge of coming up with a solution. This is how designers and planners feel when they are working on the prototype of a solution. That sense of discomfort means your subconscious mind is working on a solution that your conscious mind is not able to tackle. You tell your conscious mind to move shapes around on a piece of paper to keep it busy and focused on a task, while your subconscious mind churns away on the real problem.

Creativity is like that. When we prototype solutions, we're not necessarily coming up with the solutions. Our subconscious mind does that for us in the background as it synthesizes all the inputs we have given it along the way. There are too many factors at play when dealing with complexity for our conscious mind to grapple with. Instead of oversimplifying matters and causing even more problems, the creative process enables us to put our subconscious mind to work for us. For those not accustomed to harnessing their creativity at work, this can be uncomfortable. We have to step into the river and find that first stone. Then the next. Then the next.

As you explore possible alignments and create potential coalitions, you'll start to see patterns that become clearer. Eventually, you will come to a solution that will hit you right between the eyes. The hallmark of a good creative solution is uncovering the obvious and making the complicated simple. You have arrived when you can see a clear way for the different Influencers and Drivers to find common ground. If you need to combine them into larger groups to accomplish it, then do so. Just make sure that the groups have an air of reality to them so that you can see a way to persuading them to align if they are not currently aligned.

Driver-to-Driver Commonalities and Threads

Once you start getting a glimmer of an idea of how the Influencers and Drivers can align, the next step is to find ways for the Drivers to find that common ground. They will likely never stop being directly opposed to each other, but if you can find a way to use the leverage that the Influencers have on them and enfold them within those coalitions to the point that they have more benefit to participating than opposing, then you might be able to get back to more healthy patterns of interaction. I would recommend Coleman, et al.,[37] for more background and detail on conflict mapping.

Example from Northern Gateway

After applying this approach to Northern Gateway, there were two coalition groups that presented themselves from the data. There was a group that was primarily focused on marine protection, and a group focused on GHG emissions. If one were to draw a Venn diagram of those groups, as in Figure 1, the common participants in both groups would be the federal government, Enbridge, ENGOs, and the producers. Each of those expressed motivation to address those two key issues. More importantly, the directing minds of each of those organizations had indicated and demonstrated that interest. Keep in mind that we're focusing on patterns of behavior between individuals.

The directing minds of the groups mostly focused on GHG emissions of the upstream production was the Alberta government, where the producers were located. Those focused primarily on marine protection were the British Columbia government and the coastal Indigenous groups, particularly those who were not situated along the route and therefore bore the risk of spills without any mitigating economic upside.

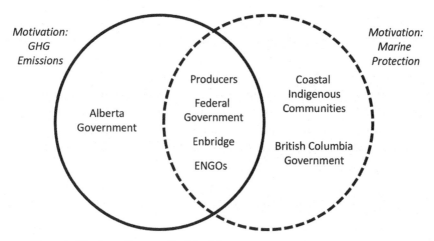

Figure 1: Northern Gateway Coalition Map

When I mapped out the conflict by common motivations, opportunities for coalition building started to present themselves. The parties were obviously not in alignment, but on these issues, neither were they in 180-degree opposition on all fronts. That's where the opportunities arose. At the time of my research, the producers, the Alberta government, and NGOs had been working together towards the common purpose of reaching GHG reduction targets. Back then, the level of cooperation between those three groups (and their directing minds) was unprecedented, and that was a viable opportunity for the federal government to show leadership in bringing them together with the other main motivation: protecting the marine environment.

On the coastal side of the equation, there were opportunities for the British Columbia government to support the Indigenous coastal communities in their primary concern of protecting their at-risk natural environment. This was also true of their secondary concern of not having the potential to achieve any economic advantage from the project because they were not situated on the pipeline route itself. One example of this that came up was a joint federal-provincially funded spill mitigation program that trained individuals and staffed stations throughout the coastal region with emergency disaster mitigation facilities. There are thousands of ships that ply those waters, and disaster mitigation was not only relevant to this project. Had the directing minds in the federal government, Enbridge, the producers, and ENGOs been able to find enough common cause on those two fronts, there may well have been enough momentum in favor of the project to allow the regulatory process to proceed as planned.

In terms of our analysis, you can see how building coalitions by finding real commonalities and perceived threads can work at the level of individuals as well as groups. The next stage for your own solution will be to map the individuals involved in the actual decision making for each of the noted organizations.

Now it's time to get persuasive.

Being Persuasive

Persuasion in the context of conflicts is different from other contexts, including negotiations. Recall that with complex conflicts, sometimes you need to aim for lose-lose instead of win-win. We're not positioning ourselves; we're shaking up patterns of interaction. We've talked about the importance of nudges over home runs and the fact that persuasion is an important element of reinvigorating dried-up patterns of interaction. Now would be a good time to put some more specifics around that.

We experience the world through the eyes of an individual, not from a group or collective. We may participate in a group, but we are only capable of experiencing it from our own perspective. We do things because they are in our own interest. We do altruistic things because we think they are right, and doing the right thing makes us feel good. We help others because it makes us feel good. We make self-sacrifices because, in the long run, it makes us happy to do things for others. In the final analysis, we do things because we look after our own needs and our own survival. Where that overlaps with the needs and benefits of others, so much the better.

We also can sublimate or postpone our immediate benefit for something in the long term. Doing this accomplishes a few things. It speaks to the very core of who we all are as humans. We look after ourselves first and foremost, and then we are free to look after others. When you give someone something, you address their most basic, unspoken concern: looking after themselves. That will help you overcome resistance to what you are about to suggest. It also helps signal to that person that you have thought about their needs and interests, and you have something they might find compelling. You have not demonstrated that yet, but you will have set the stage for when you do. It also can surprise people, particularly those with whom you participate in a conflict. Giving something first—before we ask for anything—can dramatically change the patterns of interaction. If someone's actions are consistent with a certain trajectory, and you want to change that trajectory, change the patterns of interaction that may be driving their current behavior. Shaking things up in a positive way is a potent tool for driving new behavior. Plus, it just feels great.

Persuasion can be a very effective pattern changer. It changes your own thought patterns and how you approach other participants. Thinking about how to persuade people how to change their perceptions is the first step to changing your own patterns of thinking and behaving. With this in mind, how can we persuade participants to think and feel the way we want them to? I will offer my perspective, but the point of Focal Thinking is not only to be more persuasive in a conflict but also to help you make sense of the conflict and what is driving it so that you can choose where your efforts will be the most effective. A problem well-articulated is a problem half solved, and by applying the Focal Thinking approach, you will have a much better idea of where the actual problem within a complex conflict lies. Most leaders, advisors, and conflict participants are already persuasive communicators. That said, I will offer my recommendations on the subject, based on the relevant scientific literature on complexity in conflict and on my own experience.

As I will keep saying, if you want someone to do something for you, the best way is to give them something first, before you ask for what you want. Give to get. We know that we make decisions based on emotion as well as reason, so you must be able to address the emotional elements involved in the decision you are asking someone to make. To understand the emotional aspects of the decisions you want them to make, you have to get inside their head. That is where the true work of persuasive communications happens. It is not about clever words or nice pictures; it is about knowing what drives your target and what they need to feel and think.

This might be a common approach in marketing or corporate communications, but in the context of conflicts, it is rare. The emotional and values-heavy nature of most conflicts prevents most participants from being willing to take the time to care about the emotional and rational needs of others. As a leader, advisor, or conflict participant that has learned Focal Thinking, however, you now have the advantage of clarity. With this clarity comes focus, dispassion, and an understanding of how to rise above the emotional complexity of a conflict. You have a healthy distance, as well as a laser-sharp focus on what needs to happen.

It's also rare because companies who make things, really big things, that are not destined for direct consumers are not always the best at persuasion on a large scale, because their businesses don't depend on it. Or at least in the past, it hasn't. It's just not part of their core offering. As I mentioned earlier, consumer packaged goods companies have this down to a literal science because they live and die on their ability to persuade people to use their products in highly competitive environments. They do this by finding ways to create emotional connections with their product; and those emotions drive purchase intent. It's hard to generate positive emotions around a power line, or a dam, or a mine, or other larger projects. It's much easier to generate negative ones, and that's a big point of vulnerability. Organizations and companies that create large projects, the kind that are vulnerable to complex conflicts, are not always equipped to be persuasive on a large scale. That is no longer sufficient in this day and age of empowered protest and regulatory uncertainty. The "non-technical requirements" of a project have never been more critical, and this is leaving companies flat-footed and ill-equipped to cope with the changes.

We should stop for a moment and realize what we are about to do. We are here, in the midst of a book on conflict, talking about persuasion. You may not have even noticed how unusual that is. Most approaches to conflict are about the development, use, and deployment of power. We are certainly talking about powerful tools that will accomplish what is necessary, but we are not talking about power for the sake of power. What you will end up discovering is that your role in the Focal Thinking process will be the dispenser of good things. Once you have discovered what the participants need to get and find ways to provide (or facilitate) value to them on that basis, you will find yourself in the role of value creation, which of course, is the essence of lasting persuasion.

Persuasion is a process, not an end state. It is a process that creates clarity of action: when everyone knows what to do, when to do it, and how they contribute to the larger goals of the team, organization, conflict, or overall system. The following is a useful roadmap for ensuring that you are able to persuade others by delivering value to them in the right way, at the right time. To keep things grounded, we will include practical application from the Northern Gateway example, specifically looking at how we might encourage the federal government to support the project on the point of GHG reduction.

1. Simplify

Communication involves the art and science of focus. Like a sculptor removing stone that obscures the true sculpture, a communicator removes the noise and gets to the heart of the matter by breaking it down to its simplest components. You are now able to accomplish this using your new way of approaching complexity using the Focal Thinking process, which helps you find elegant simplicity you can use right away. In the Northern Gateway example, we identified the fact that the Conflict Drivers were the federal government and the proponent, and we mapped out a series of Influencers (the Alberta government, the producers, and specific environmental groups). We also found ways to approach aligning the various interests to the point that they might be willing to engage effectively.

2. Clarify

Elegant simplicity is only useful if people understand what it means to them, in their world. To bring that to life when solving a persuasion challenge, the people involved need to see the elegantly simple root of the challenge, engage with what that means to them, and get to the point where they understand it themselves. In the case of Northern Gateway, most participants were fully aware of what it meant to them from their own perspective, but not necessarily from the standpoint of others. As you map out your persuasion strategy, it will be essential to include in your analysis what might be missing from the perception of the participants as it relates to the others. From the Northern Gateway example, where the producers, environmental groups, and the provincial government already came together over a mutual interest in reducing GHG emissions, it might have been the case that the federal government was not fully aware of the scope and depth of that alignment. Depending on the timing of the situation, they might not have had the opportunity to flesh out the federal-level policy implications of that province-level alignment. Preparing your persuasion strategy to accomplish that clarity might be a key element to changing the patterns of interaction and perception in just the right way.

3. Serve

Serve first, then ask. As I mentioned, in this approach, the key to getting people to do what you want them to do is to first give them what they need before they even ask for it. Perceptual challenges often come up when people prioritize what they want over what they need. At this stage, you need to force people to grapple with the difference and acknowledge the fact they won't always get what they want. Taking the previous example a step further, the federal government not only needed to know what the federal-level policy implications of the environmental/producer/province alignment were, but they also needed to see what was in it for them. If that group were to proactively recommend policy implications that would further a federal agenda item—related to Northern Gateway or not—they might be able to create a new pattern of interaction that would open the door to supporting the project.

It is vital to keep adding value, even after the first time. If your follow-through is not consistent, your lead-up will falter. A tennis swing must be a beautiful arc from start to contact to finish. If the finish is off, the contact will be wrong, and the ball will not go where you want it to go. The same has been true in the world of sales since the beginning of human economic activity. Post-purchase satisfaction is a critical part of the overall sale and brands that understand that create better experiences for customers. This creates brand advocates and increases the likelihood of repeat purchases. It is part of fundamental human nature that we want to feel good about a purchase decision that we have made. The same principle applies when persuading people to take action in a workplace situation. This is particularly important in implementing the kind of disruptive design solutions we are talking about. Not just because we want to generate continued goodwill, but because it is very easy for anyone to reverse their decision at any point. In complex conflicts, a *yes* is never permanent. Neither is a *no*.

It's also important to remember that we're shaking up patterns of interaction. What better way to shake up how someone has stereotyped you by authentically showing up with something of value, unasked?

4. Engage

We know that conflicts are driven and perpetuated by broken, missing, or dried-up patterns of interaction. Once we know what people need, we can find ways to create new constructive patterns of interaction, or we can shake up existing destructive ones. These patterns are designed to create the kind of healthy engagement that will start motivating people to do what we need them to do. Now is the time for action. You already know how to effectively engage with people. What you may not have known is the how and why of a value persuasion approach. The one thing I would remind you of at this point is the fact that everything communicates. Everything you say, everything you do, and even everything you think. It all ends up in the conflict system at some point. While that can be a daunting prospect that will keep you your guard, it also opens up a wide range of opportunities for how you chose to engage participants.

Following along with our example, say that the Alberta coalition has studied the federal-level policy recommendations and developed some interesting ideas for how the federal government could make use of that to their advantage. You could communicate that in any number of ways. If the relevant politicians would need to appear at arm's length because of a few green-leaning constituent bases, you could communicate it through a neutral third party or by helping mobilize other Influencers in a peripherally-related matter—such as the British Columbia government on matters related to coastal marine protection. In persuasion, anything is possible when you recognize that everything communicates.

5. Mobilize

Make it easy for people to do what you want. Once you see that patterns of interaction are producing constructive, useful engagement, you want to make sure they are taking the action you want them to take. This involves making sure people understand what you want them to do, making it easy for them to do it, and continuously improving that process, so more and more action will result. Once participants are doing what you need them to do, they know why they're doing it, and they see the benefit, the system perpetuates itself. This means you absolutely must have clearly-articulated steps they can take to help you. The worst thing you can do in the value-based persuasion approach is to leave people hanging once you have them favorably disposed to what you want. Make it clear and easy for them.

Going back to our example, you would need to do everything possible to make it easy for the federal government to provide support for the project. You might broker meetings where the proponent and federal government officials are both in attendance. You might create joint task forces where they collaborate on other related matters, such as the marine protection issue. Or perhaps they are completely unrelated matters such as the arts, culture or sports, or similar areas in which everyone can be comfortable finding common ground in a neutral environment. The point is that you will need to make it very easy for people to engage with the right people in a new way. Those new patterns of interaction will be what break down the barriers.

As you start thinking differently about the where, how, why, and what of conflicts, you also will start thinking differently about your role. An effective way to change patterns of interaction in a conflict is to use value-delivering persuasion, and the Focal Thinking approach will help make that happen.

Facilitated Engagement

Another step on our tactical consideration list is facilitated engagements. There are going to be lots of opportunities to get people engaged on a formal basis, and anything you can do on this front is going to be critical to the process. This is something that most companies are good at. Robust engagement teams are now more the rule than the exception, and this is a good thing. The root of the issue is not the team's capability, but how they are deployed and the scope of their mandate.

There are still companies and organizations that use engagement as persuasion rather than as part of their strategic deliberation process. If a company treats its stakeholders and potential antagonists as co-creators within a project as it's being developed and planned, the chances of sustained opposition are much less, and the risks go down. This is a particularly sensitive issue in countries with Indigenous populations and their right to be consulted. As the UN Declaration on the Rights of Indigenous Peoples slowly makes its way into domestic legislative frameworks, this will only become more common. The challenge is often not in creating opportunities for consultative engagement but deciding who needs to be engaged. When you have populations that are semi-autonomous with differing governance structures, that can be challenging. One client had undertaken significant consultation along their project route and gained the support of the elected officials in all the impacted Indigenous groups, only to have some members within those groups claim the right to be consulted because the elected officials were not legitimate authorities under their interpretation of their own territorial laws. A press hungry for scandal and eager to take the side of the perceived underdog took that and made an issue out of it.

But what about after the horse has left the barn and we're in a full-blown conflict, long after the initial consultations are completed? Can facilitated engagement still play a role? If we remember that a conflict is about perceptions, and our goal is to shake up existing patterns of interaction, then the answer is yes. Of course it can. In fact, I would argue that facilitated engagement should be an enduring feature of any large project, from start to finish. Unless you can promise that nothing will ever go wrong after the initial round of engagement (which you can't), having a standing series of engagements will be a great idea because it will force the patterns of interaction to stay open. Think of it like an IV line during a medical operation. Sometimes you need it for important things like anesthetic or blood, and sometimes you need it for a saline solution to keep hydrated. Either way, you want to have it there and ready at a moment's notice. More than one client I've worked with has a standing meeting with key stakeholders who meet regularly whether there's an issue or not. Having that positive momentum is valuable in itself, and it also makes it easier to deal with matters as they arise, without having to be seen to be calling a "special meeting," which can often make a smallish matter look more significant than it is.

Facilitated engagement is something most large companies and organizations are good at, so the question is where, when and how to deploy that important function throughout the course of a project in order to shake up any potentially problematic interactions. More is better.

The Role of Research

We talked about the importance of doing up-front research to create our Human Landscape Model, but how will we know if our pattern shakeups are working? Do we need to do research along the way to keep an eye on things? I'll declare one of my biases right now: I am a big fan of research, and it's a big part of how I earn a living. That said, you'll need to be very careful about doing research at this stage. Let's take a step back for a minute and think about this. Remember, we're now in the perception business. In our approach, we create coalitions based on the commonalities and threads between and among the Conflict Influencers and Drivers, so we can help them perceive our ideal future state as being the one they also will prefer, or at least allow. To accomplish that change in their perception means persuading them, and those persuasion goals will drive our strategy.

Key questions that often come up with creative persuasion strategies are; how do we know what people think now? How will we know when they have been persuaded? The good news is that to get this far along, you will have already laid the groundwork. Your planned future state is based on what people think and feel already. You might need to validate it along the way with some direct or third-party qualitative research to make sure you are not missing anything, but you couldn't have developed your prototype without a keen understanding of the perceptual drivers involved. Using the Northern Gateway example, after mapping out the prototype, you could either engage a research company to confirm your findings as they relate to the motivations of the participants, or you could have someone with knowledge of the players involved provide their perspective.

The challenge to be careful of is that you do not impact the system by the action of sampling for information. Recall that we are part of the overall conflict system, and our actions have an impact, just as much as any Conflict Influencer or Driver. We are not observing from a lofty ivory tower; we are actually in the conflict. This means that everything you do communicates something. By approaching one of the players with a question about their perspective on your new prototype, you will have related something new to them that may have an impact beyond what you expected. Using the Northern Gateway example, if you directly asked an environmental group if they willing to support the producers in helping to create an alliance with coastal Indigenous groups and the British Columbia government, you may or may not find out their perspective depending on how you gathered your information. However, you will have communicated the fact that this is a possible strategy for your prototype, and now they know exactly what you are thinking, without the benefit of a layer of persuasive communication to help ensure you get what you want from them.

There are no neutral actions. Everything communicates, including research. That doesn't mean you shouldn't use research to validate your perspective. It means that you need to realize that the act of sampling for data can have ramifications in and of itself. Recall the section where I briefly mentioned the conflict in which the researchers discovered that just by using Q Methodology, they were able to change the outcome of the conflict. That methodology involved having the participants actively engage with each other's perceptions of the conflict in a neutral, safe, non-confrontational environment. Ostensibly it was to help the researchers gather information on the various perceptions, but it also ended up changing the perceptions of the participants only by their engagement in the research process itself. If you use research, you need to be sure to use it as a communication tool as well as an information-gathering tool.

Another factor is much more practical. You can research anything you want to if you have the money to do it. Like the lawyer asking her client how much justice he can afford, the question you need to ask is, how much knowledge can you afford? Continually going back to the well for more and more information gets very expensive, and at some point, you will need to do a cost-benefit analysis to see how important it is in comparison to the alternative uses of the money. You may find it will be more useful to spend money on engagement sessions than constantly asking people if your strategy is working. Since this is a game of constant nudges rather than big wins, in theory, you could spend a lot of time chasing this information, and by the time the data come in, you may need to be on to the next nudge.

I hesitate to bring this up, but research won't always work in this context. You can only ask people about things in which they have some expertise, including their own feelings, thoughts, and perspectives. But when you are trying to persuade people to do things, they don't always have the self-awareness to be able to tell you anything useful. For example, if you ask people whether they are influenced by a particular piece of communication or advertising, they invariably say no. Nobody wants to admit that advertising influences them, even though their behavior says otherwise. If you have to ask if your strategy is working, you're not always going to get a straight answer.

I strongly recommend that you do your own eyes-open research. You've created a Human Landscape Model that has lots of information in it about motivations, perspectives, and likely next steps. Let that be your research tool, and just keep your eyes open at all times, keeping that model updated. But be sure to be honest with yourself and others that you are biased, you have skin in the game, and everything you see and do is going to be colored by that fact. There's nothing wrong with that as long as you work hard to get as broad a perspective as possible and make sure you're incorporating all the competing perspectives and interests. What you can't allow yourself to do is pretend that you're unbiased and neutral. That's dishonest and inaccurate. And it's unnecessary. We're all biased; so declare it, own it, and do your best to capture everything you see to keep that model updated. We'll talk more about this in the last segment on staying resilient.

Wrap-Up and What's Next

Now you have some new ways to think about how you might reinvigorate the dried-up patterns of interaction you're going to find in a complex conflict. That is going to be a big part of your ability to show strategic leadership because you'll be able to clearly explain what needs to happen next, and why. My favorite part of this process is focusing on how to add value and give to those who may not be expecting it. What a great way to shake things up, and what a great feeling to bring to what is probably otherwise an unpleasant situation. Many of these are skills you already have, or that your team has, available to you. But when you think about them as pattern shake-ups in a world of nudges, not home runs, it can change how you put those to use.

Next, we are going to cover something that gets very little attention: how to be persuasive in the office, once you've solved all the problems of the world.

Be Persuasive in the Office

I see this all the time, where the issues management team and those on the ground see what needs to happen to move things forward, but when it comes time to mobilizing head office, they run into a brick wall. The inconvenient human complexity does not play well with the folks who never have to put on work boots just to have a meeting, or sit in front of an angry community association, or bear the brunt of a frustrated protester. They need help understanding what needs to happen, and to do that, you're going to need to make sure you're as persuasive with head office as you are with Conflict Drivers and Influencers.

It's essential for you and the team on the ground dealing with the issues to come up with solutions, but if they are unable to be persuasive in the office, then those changes may run into implementation roadblocks. Being persuasive with coworkers carries an additional layer of changes that we will want to cover now. We're going to talk about the inherently disruptive nature of designing solutions and how you might be able to put a twist on change management principles to increase your persuasive abilities in the office.

Implementing Your Solutions

Our earlier discussion of design thinking will help us with this challenge. Remember, by "design," we mean the collaborative process by which we find our way to workable solutions using the principles of abductive reasoning. We're crossing that river, not with a bridge (deduction) or with a catapult (induction), but by crossing it in a zig-zag line one stone at a time.

When you get on a highway, you want to minimize the disruption to the cars already there. The goal is to use the on-ramp to get up to speed so that when it comes time to merge onto the highway, you are going the same speed as the others. The most dangerous thing you can do is to try to enter the road going too slowly because that disrupts the traffic flow and forces other drivers to guess what you are trying to do. They will either have to slow down to avoid a collision or swerve out of your way. Roads work best when everyone is going roughly the same speed.

The same principle applies at work. When you show up with a newly designed solution, if you're not mindful of how it will impact others, you are behaving like the person who blunders onto a six-lane speedway going 30 mph. In the best scenario, you will force others to swerve, slam on their brakes, panic, or all of the above. In the worst scenario, you will get run over by people who cannot, will not, or need not change direction. In the most likely scenario, you and your ideas are going to be run off the road, and all your hard work will be for nothing.

Any type of design solution is normative, so it is also disruptive by nature. When we design things, including solutions to complex conflicts, we are drawing a line in the sand. We're saying what should be (that's what "normative" means) and what should not be. We're making choices. We can't have everything, and so we make decisions about what should happen and what should not happen. This is part of providing strategic leadership - knowing what to do next and why to do it. This is also disruptive to the status quo, and disruption is difficult for people. It is easy to disrupt others, but it is uncomfortable being disrupted, even if that disruption is in your own best interest. This is critical to remember when you use Focal Thinking or any type of designed disruption because Focal Thinkers often suffer from the Cassandra complex. This refers to the Greek myth in which Cassandra was able to see the future but suffered because nobody believed her. Focal Thinkers aren't prognosticating the future, we're inventing it. We're making the desired future come into being, and doing so by using a different type of thinking than most are used to. This will be uncomfortable for many others, and making people uncomfortable is not always a great way to advance your career or to make friends. This section will give you some insights into how to wield your new-found power to maximum benefit to others and minimal damage to yourself.

Before we dive in, it's important to note that a great deal of ink has been spilled over the years on innovation, design thinking, and organizational impact. What I will be suggesting from this point forward are recommendations based on my experience and that of others. However, you are more than welcome to substitute your own approaches to getting things done at work. If you're a leader or advisor, you will undoubtedly be more than competent in this area. If you're a conflict participant, that may or may not be the case, depending on your background. In either case, there is one thing that is not optional: To implement Focal Thinking, you absolutely must be intentional about it. Otherwise, you'll be providing yet another layer of patterns of interaction in the midst of a large complex system. If you are not measured, intentional, and strategic about applying Focal Thinking, you won't be adding anything new to the conflict.

Since you will likely have your own approaches to implementing plans, strategies, and projects at work, I'll focus on the critical considerations you'll need to be aware of along the way. Like any design solution, Focal Thinking will require you to account for some possibly new factors as you develop your approach to implementation. In addition to pointing out some new pitfalls you'll face, I will also provide suggestions from my experience and the experience of those who have successfully addressed these challenges. You are free to pick and choose what will work in your context. You are not, unfortunately, free to ignore the fact that Focal Thinking will bring a new set of challenges for you.

Design Is Normative

Design is normative, which is another way of saying that it involves deciding what should be. Design is a series of choices, the result of which is that which should come into existence that did not exist before. As a sculptor removes all the stone that is not the sculpture, or the Apollo 13 engineer decides which lunar module parts to use for the CO2 scrubber, designers like you make choices. Some things are in, and some things are out. Design is where we go from theoretical to practical. We can dream about something all day long, but until we make hard choices about what that something will become in real life, it will stay a dream.

Things that are normative carry values because values inform the decisions we make along the way. A website creator, for example, is faced with a myriad of decisions. They can choose to prioritize what the user wants, or they can make life easy for the IT department and prioritize what those folks need. Either way, someone is going to win something, and someone is going to lose something. And that is the challenge with designing solutions. Once things become real, people start paying attention and realize they may or may not get what they think they wanted. People who design and plan things run into this problem all the time. Once something becomes real, others start critiquing. It is human nature. It also happens because most of us are not trained to think far enough ahead to envision the outcome of a design strategy until after it starts coming to fruition.

At work, this can cause any number of challenges. One involves authority. Because you are designing a solution that should be, you are automatically taking jurisdiction over a situation. Depending on where you work, most people in the role of designing solutions are not necessarily at the top of the organizational chart. It is very easy to be seen to be overstepping your authority or usurping the authority of someone much higher than you in the food chain. This will be a compounded challenge when those in authority are not also those with the skillset or temperament to themselves be design thinkers. Say, for example, that you are designing a solution to a complex conflict, and you work for a firm whose culture places a heavy value on engineers. Your authority may be severely constrained if those responsible have been rewarded within the organization for their inductive or deductive reasoning ability. Giving decision-making authority to someone who is taking an abductive approach to a problem may well be counter to the existing culture. Senior leadership may make noise about being innovative and forward-thinking, but in their minds, they may be thinking "more of the same," not "completely new approach with which they are not familiar."

There are plenty of books on innovation, and they will tell you that if you are going to innovate as a designer bringing normative recommendations, you need to have air cover within your organization. If you are a leader, this certainly holds true. We all report to someone, and if that someone is not willing to let you have the authority to make a recommendation that takes a different approach, you'll be on shaky ground. Even if you can get agreement on the solution, you may have difficulty gaining traction. If you're a conflict advisor, the same issue applies, but in a different sense. Organizations often purposefully retain external advisors because they are free to think and recommend as they see fit, without being beholden to the corporate culture or politics. However, if the direct line into the organization you are counseling is not far enough up the food chain or suffers from a deficit in authority, your recommendations will have an uphill battle. If you're a conflict participant, you may face entirely different challenges. If you're acting on your own or are an isolated part of a complex conflict, you may not have the ability to mobilize an organization to implement or react to your designed solution. Without the ability to have influence, your designed solution will languish untested and unused.

Design is Disruptive

Not only is design normative, but it is also disruptive by nature because it changes the status quo. When it moves from paper to reality, it changes what is. Even if something is in our own best interest, disruption is challenging for us. All change can be uncomfortable, and this is particularly the case if it's imposed on us. When you put on a hat, it's comfortable. When someone puts a hat on your head, the first thing you do is adjust it, even if it was in exactly the same spot.

A designed solution can disrupt us for many reasons. It can require us to change our behavior. If we are creating new patterns of interaction to change the course of a complex conflict, then that is exactly what we are asking people to do. Changing behavior is never a simple matter, and without a strategy in place, your ability to implement a conflict course correction is going to be very limited.

Designed solutions are also disruptive because, unless you can convince others to change on their own accord, imposed change can feel demeaning; like an exertion of power. Regardless of the source of authority or the eventual benefit to all involved, a disruptive design can feel like an infringement on the autonomy of the people involved. Recall from our earlier discussion about the role of emotion and non-rational behavior in complex conflicts. Participants in longstanding conflicts often stay involved when it is not actually in their own best interest. Asking someone in that frame of mind to disrupt their behavior is an incendiary objective that is very likely to meet with resistance at best, and hostility at worst.

As a leader, you will be familiar with organizational change and the impact of managing conflict. Leaders who are not clear that their ideas, no matter how outstanding, are disruptive by nature will not rise as far as they otherwise might. Conflict advisors similarly need to know that their ideas are going to be disruptive and difficult for somebody along the way, and a strategy to change patterns of interaction that does not include tactics to manage the disruption is doomed to fail. Participants may be more attuned to the disruptive nature of their design solution since they are intimately connected to their particular conflict. You're going to want to make sure the change management aspect of your effort is front-and-center in the tactical execution of your strategy.

When getting traction for innovations within an organization, be aware that the solutions are going to be normative and, therefore, will cause resistance. Just because smart people can design a workable solution to a conflict does not mean other people will fall in line. That is obvious. But the underlying reason may not be. The normative and disruptive nature of your designed solution needs to be at the forefront of your mind as you plan strategies for implementation. If conflict is the perception of incompatible activities, that perception drives entrenched patterns of behavior that will not easily yield to change; at least not without a clear plan. Making this even more poignant, your design solutions will be evolving as constantly as your conflict changes, so your disruptions will not be one-time transactions. As a Focal Thinker, you are about to show up at work as a source of constant, ongoing, persistent disruption. Are you ready for that?

Using Organizational Change Management

Organizational Change Management (OCM) is usually associated with technology implementation, but it can also be a helpful starting point when looking at ways to implement your new way of thinking in the office. You will find that it is helpful, but there are shortcomings and limits to its application to dynamic conflicts, so it's going to need a few enhancements. Nonetheless, it's a good place to start the process of thinking about how to implement your ideas.

OCM assumes that you can lead a horse to water, but you can't make him drink. OCM provides a structured way to ensure you are providing the people whose patterns of behavior you want to change with the value they need before you ask them to change. Change needs to be managed, and disruptive change needs to be managed very carefully and intentionally. If you don't have a plan to intentionally manage the implementation of the change you want to see, your likelihood of success is lower than it could be. If you are not familiar with the field of organizational change management, you owe it to yourself to learn as much as possible. If you hope to implement disruptive design solutions (a redundant phrase if there ever was one), then you'll need to be conversant in at least one approach to change management. This next section will be a helpful overview of some of the central tenets involved.

There are many different approaches, but I tend to gravitate to OCM because it is rooted in technology implementation and is, therefore, quite practical and methodical. In many ways, it brings the process and rigor of a project management approach to something that otherwise runs the risk of being nebulous, opaque, and—speaking frankly—a bit squishy. The other benefit of drawing on a formal approach like OCM is that the process itself can lend credibility to your design solution. This is especially the case when your internal audience is familiar with the process in a different context. Find what they are familiar with, and serve it back to them in terms of they already know. For example, if the company you lead, or the clients you serve, or your fellow conflict participants are engineers, you will be well served to speak a language with which they are already familiar. If your plan can fit within the constraints of an approach like OCM, for example, this has the benefit of ensuring your plan is feasible, and it will make it easier for those being asked to buy into it. There are, however, some limitations to using the OCM approach to implementing design solutions at work, and I will note these as we go along.

One classic OCM approach is Kotter's[38] 8-Step process for leading change. Here are the eight steps and how they might apply to a complex conflict.

1. Establish a Sense of Urgency

Kotter's first step involves creating a sense of urgency to the new patterns of behavior you will be trying to implement. You might think that a conflict already carries a sense of urgency, but that is not the point. The goal is to create a sense of urgency around the change itself, not the existing conflict. This is one of the most challenging steps. Recall that from the theoretical framework of nonlinear dynamical systems, a complex conflict is actually a stable system. It may be negative, destructive, and dynamic, but it is stable in the sense that it's not going away any time soon. The Coherence Trap tells us it's stable because people have oversimplified their patterns of interaction to help them act despite all the uncomfortable complexity. If we're going to get people to change their patterns of interaction when they're very comfortable in the current ones, it's going to be a challenge to create a sense of urgency to encourage those changes. Here are some ideas to create this sense of urgency.

One way to create urgency around a new pattern of behavior is to create it yourself. We talked about the persuasion philosophy of getting people to do things for you by giving them something first before you ask. That is a good example of leading the change you want to see. Taking responsibility for your side of the street and changing your own patterns of interaction is an excellent way to create a sense of urgency in others to do the same. Creating a sense of "urgency" does not necessarily mean creating an "emergency." All we need to do is instill motivation in others to be open to change. When they see others changing first, that can be a powerful motivator. If not to change immediately, at least to be open to the idea of changing. Another way to create a sense of openness to change is to encourage those in more direct contact than you to lead the change. There will be times when you have no direct contact with those whose patterns of interaction need to change. Your task, in this case, will be to find those Influencers who can be directly influential and encourage them to change their approach. This takes us to the next step, which relates to coalitions.

2. Create the Guiding Coalition

The second step in Kotter's approach is to create a guiding coalition, and this will be familiar to us because it's part of our approach to shaking up interactions in the conflict itself, not just in the office. Nothing signals changing behavior like a group of people changing at once. Recall our discussion of Conflict Influencers, Fisher and Ury's "third side," and the approach of using them to get leverage on those who are in more direct opposition to each other. By creating a group of conflict participants who have overlapping interests, even if they are not entirely aligned, you can create an influential coalition to get leverage on those most problematic to the conflict. This approach works with conflicts, and it also works within your organization. Like my colleague from military psychological operations said, there will be those who are directly opposed to your recommended course of action, those in indirect opposition, and those in support. You can use the same type of analysis you would in a complex conflict and create your coalitions to gain support.

3. Develop a Vision and Strategy

According to Kotter, the next stage is to develop a vision and strategy. In our quest, we will have already created our vision and strategy for the conflict itself, using the Focal Thinking process. The point here is to develop a vision and strategy for getting our conflict strategy implemented at work. A strategy to implement a strategy, if you will. It seems counterintuitive to leave this to the third stage of the OCM process, and you may well want to have this planned out in advance. However, it can be useful to do so after you have created a sense of urgency and created the guiding coalition because doing so will help you generate the buy-in you are going to need. Independent of the strategy you develop, if you develop it together with your coalition, they'll have skin in the game and will be much more willing and able to provide the kind of support you will need with the rest of the organization.

4. Communicate the Change Vision

People will not think their way to change; they need to feel it first. What we learned about decision making in conflicts being grounded in both emotion *and* reason also applies to situations where we expect others to change. Change is disruptive and unsettling, even if it is good for us, and to encourage people to get past that, you will need to provide a compelling vision of the future you want them to help create. As a leader, advisor, or conflict participant, you probably already are adept at getting your vision across to others. What I would strongly recommend, however, is that you use the same value persuasion approach at work as you developed in your Focal Thinking strategy. Not only will this help you get what you want, but it will set you up for all the times your vision will change throughout the course of the conflict. Remember, as we discussed in the previous section, those changes are going to be a constant feature of your approach. This will be an additional challenge to all those around you who will constantly be disrupted. You will need their goodwill, and you will need it regularly, not only as a one-time transaction.

5. Empower Employees for Broad-Based Action

Kotter emphasized the importance of empowering employees, and this cannot be overstated. As I mentioned earlier, strategy is what happens after the consultants have submitted their invoices (my favorite part) and folks have to implement all the new stuff. If the strategy is sound and clearly, compellingly articulated, they will know what to do next. If not, all the strategic planning in the world will not accomplish much. Once you and your guiding coalition have a clear vision that is ready to be well-told, it is time to take it on the road for a broader audience. This consistent pipeline of action will be critical as you continuously evolve your conflict approach. Not only must they be willing, but they must also have the relational infrastructure to continually adapt and adjust to new data and strategy.

6. Generate Short-Term Wins

The proof of the pudding, as they say, is in the taste. At this point, you need to make sure that you accomplish some quick wins, or better yet, empower others to do so. This is imperative at the early stage because unless you can demonstrate success immediately, your strategy will never make it off the paper and into people's lives. This is where you want to find a component of your Focal Thinking strategy that will lend itself to picking some low-hanging fruit (or slow-moving meat, if you're a carnivore).

The point of your Focal Thinking strategy is to change patterns of interaction to accomplish the larger purpose of helping a conflict become constructive and avoid being destructive. We know from our nonlinear dynamical systems theory that we are unlikely to affect a system change immediately—although it is not impossible—so the goal of any short-term win should not be to change the system but to demonstrate your team's ability to change patterns of interaction. If you can take a specific pattern that leans to the destructive side of the equation, and you know there is a way to change that pattern, consider making that your first short-term win. If you can help the team create that first change, they will see that it is possible. Furthermore, it can be a great feeling when you see the impact of one small change.

7. Consolidate Gains and Produce More Change

Once you have momentum with a quick win, you're going to want to keep that momentum moving. Kotter suggests that you consolidate the gains from the quick win and use it to produce more change. Nothing creates success like a previous success. In our case, if you can show the wider team the impact of the change in interaction patterns you just created, and demonstrate the impact of that small win, you can use that to spur others on to action because they will know it can be done and will have seen how to do it.

8. Anchor New Approaches in the Culture

The main challenge with OCM as a discipline is rooted in its origins. It has traditionally been used to implement new organizational changes or technology, which are linear projects. They have a start date, an implementation timeline, an end date, and a maintenance schedule. While the components of an OCM approach are helpful, the idea that you can sequentially work your way out of a conflict is the type of thinking that contributed to the conflict in the first place. Keep that up, and you're going to land right back in the Coherence Trap you worked so hard to get out of. That's why at the final stages of your implementation plan, you will need to build a culture of resilience that will continuously evaluate and re-evaluate previous strategies and decisions. We'll talk in-depth about that in the next section.

Once you have created a series of successes, you will want to embed those changes into the culture. There are a number of ways to do this, depending on the culture. If you have a process-driven culture, change the processes to fit your new learnings. If you have a relationship-driven culture, give the most influential people a platform to talk about the successes and what it meant to them. An excellent way to embed a new approach in any culture is to a post-mortem of the project, couched in the terminology of a hand-off to the next team of implementers. Once they see it as a hand-off, you already have won, because the term itself assumes you have already adopted what the team is developing—before you even hold the first meeting.

Dealing with Boards

So what about your bosses? How can we use Focal Thinking to manage upward? This is all well and good for teams that you lead, but what about when you have other executives or board members demanding results? The key is going to be keeping them focused on the process too, so you're going to want to give them something solid to pay attention to. Most corporate boards have risk management committees, or at least have that function spread across a few committees. Let's give them something to do, so they can participate and even contribute. Normally, getting boards involved in management activities is to be avoided at all costs, but there may be some ways they can be useful in the right ways.

A good start is the risk register, which is a running list of risks identified within the organization. Management uses this to keep the board abreast of the risks they find and are working to resolve. This mechanism helps the board fulfill their duty to guide the organization. But in a complex, dynamic situation the risk register ends up being more of a historical record that a meaningful tool. By the time you would have developed today's strategy and added it to the register, you will have been aiming for the next one already. When the board has their quarterly update, the risk register will be little more than an interesting but irrelevant record of the past. How can you expect to generate support and momentum for your conflict strategies when you can't generate a proper level of visibility for your superiors?

One approach is to give them the right level of detail. Consider creating a subcommittee tasked with convening for "emergent" matters, and give them a policy, guideline or procedure to formally follow. That will mandate their attention on a timely basis, and put some firewalls around the scope of their engagement. As an example, consider a "Conflict Risk Register" that maps out all the Conflict Drivers who currently have power, but avoids delving into the Conflict Influencers and your detailed strategies. This will enable the board to have visibility into your challenges at a high level without getting bogged down in daily operations. This can also help galvanize and utilize any connections the board might have. Most board members are well-connected and influential in their own right. If that can be of value when dealing with Conflict Drivers, why not take advantage of it? Not only will this advance your objective, it will help generate a practical level of engagement within a subgroup of the board. When you combine that momentum with a clear-written policy or policy amendment, it can be a very effective way of ensuring the kind of support you're going to need within the organization.

Wrap-Up and What's Next

If you can't mobilize your organization, you're going to have a hard time showing strategic leadership. Since design is normative, i.e. it's saying what *should* be rather than what is, design is inherently disruptive. Whenever you create something new, you can count on the fact that someone, somewhere, isn't going to like it. We all want to change things, but nobody wants to be changed. When we show up at the office with our Human Landscape Models and our pattern-busting persuasion strategies, we are disruptive to the status quo. This will be frustrating for those who are not used to thinking abductively, and who demand timelines and budgets and Gantt charts and deliverable expectations. All those things are essential and need to be accommodated, but in many cases, those same folks making those demands are the very same folks that put us all in the middle of a human minefield, so they're going to need to let the experts do their job. That's what you're walking into. Using some tried and true change management strategies will help you be as strategic and intentional in the office as you are with the conflict itself.

In the next and last step, we are going to look at how to stay resilient in the face of the kind of constant, dynamic change that comes with complex conflicts.

Stay Resilient

The last milestone on our obstacle/path is staying resilient. We talked about the importance of being resilient versus consistent because of the "dynamic" part of our nonlinear dynamical systems. This will mean that our team approach will need to have an extra layer of interaction to ensure that everybody stays flexible and adaptable. It's not enough to come up with tactics; we'll need to be able to jettison those tactics on a moment's notice and pivot immediately to a new opportunity. And do that regularly. This section will cover how to create the kind of team dynamic that will enable everyone to do that, and then look at some practical ways to make sure you are monitoring and adapting with agility as the conflict unfolds.

Creating the Team Dynamic

If you and your coworkers are going to keep up with constant change, you'll need to instill the right mindset. To do that, the team dynamic will need to encourage people to have the qualities that we talked about before: collaboration, humility, persuasion, and the ability to create nudges versus big wins. If you are going to bring disruption to an emotionally charged conflict, you are going to need some help. As we have discussed, the biggest impediment to making sense of complex conflicts is our own thinking: about how we know the truth about conflicts, why they behave the way they do, how they happen, and what we should measure along the way. But it's not just our own thinking that gets in the way; it's that of our teams and the people around us who are also on this journey. We thought the way we used to think about conflicts for very good reasons. To expect that we, or the teams we are involved with, are completely going to change their thought patterns because we read a book—even an outstanding book—is more than a bit presumptuous.

There are some obstacles to thinking differently that we will need to address at the outset. Some of these are related to our own thought processes, and some are related to working in teams. Keep in mind as we go through this section that an abductive, iterative, design thinking approach to problem-solving is not necessarily something that we are used to. It may be different. It may seem unusual at first. If it were otherwise, we would not expect it to accomplish a new type of result for us. Once we establish the right mindset in ourselves and our teams from the start of the sensemaking process, we will stand a much better chance of success.

Getting Your Team Ready for Design Thinking

Any design thinking approach requires collaboration on a level that most teams don't experience on a daily basis. Unless you run a design, communications, or similar innovation-driven organization, the chances are good that your team could use some extra help with this. Regardless of whether this is already the case or if your team needs some work, the following will help get them—and you—ready for the task ahead. The path won't be a straight line, and you may need to double back more than once. If you have a strong team ready to collaborate, you'll be more likely to reach the result you want. We will discuss more about the mechanics of making that happen, but for now, the purpose is to get in the right frame of mind.

If we treat the team like a system (although hopefully not a complex conflict), it will help us get our thinking organized. We now know that systems are patterns of interaction that can take on lives of their own beyond the immediate intentions of the people involved. When they turn bad, they become destructive conflicts, and when they turn good, they become virtuous cycles of creative outcomes. My days of design management was spent putting people together, establishing the rules of engagement, and watching the results take off. When I create teams, I always give them five simple rules of engagement that help create the patterns of interaction that would set the team up for successful design thinking.

1. Treat Each Other Like a Job Reference

First, treat each other like future job references. The fact is that most of our industries are relatively small, closed systems, and the chances of working together in other roles throughout the course of one's career are very high. Encourage your team members to remember this fact and act accordingly. When you look at team interactions as long-term relationships and not short-term transactions, they will tend to treat each other in a way that will support their career development. More importantly, however, they will interact in ways that support collaborative innovation. I think of this as the Uber effect. When you use Uber ride-sharing software, not only do you rate your Uber driver, but they also rate you. When you request an Uber car online, every driver can see your rating before they decide whether to pick you up or not. This puts people on their best behavior on both sides of the transaction. When you have a team that has to be cohesive, that is precisely how you want them to interact with each other. This puts people in the mindset that we all need to be continually impressing each other and be looking out for each other at every step. When you interact that way, it creates new pathways of interaction that inevitably lead to better results. As a happy by-product, it also creates a great work environment.

2. Get to Maximum Appropriate Truth

Second, they need to always get to maximum appropriate truth with each other. If something is bugging you, get it said as soon as possible because each small interaction creates ripples that take on their own lives in the larger system, often far beyond what was originally intended. Keep in mind, however, that it must be said in a way that will build the relationship in the long term (remember Rule One). This is not a license to shoot off your mouth and be hurtful under the guise of "just being honest." Truth is appropriate when it builds the relationship for the long term, understanding that there will always be bumps along the way.

3. Be a Hotbed of Ideas

Third, the team needs to see themselves as being a hotbed of ideas, so anything that gets in the way of that needs to be dealt with immediately. Things like egos, destructive behavior, failure to accommodate introverts in group settings, etc., need to be overcome, or the best idea won't bubble to the top. As a leader, you need to set the tone by acknowledging that your idea may not always be the best one, and when a better idea comes along, you have to be seen to jettison yours for the better one. Your role is to create a system where the best idea rises, not to be the smartest one in the room.

4. Prioritize Excellence

Fourth, individuals need to love excellence in what they are doing or creating together. Here is why: As I mentioned, strategy is what happens in the small moments when nobody is looking. If every single person is passionate about what the group is doing, they will guard against anything that will water it down or cause it to be less than amazing.

5. Leverage the Chain of Command

Fifth, the group needs to understand, respect, and leverage the chain of command. Each system has a hierarchy, whether it's overt or unspoken. If the role of someone with responsibility for others is to make their team's work-life easier by removing barriers and bringing clarity, it's the responsibility of the team members to make sure that happens. The hardest challenge for a leader is getting accurate, timely information, and if the team can provide that information, it has an enormous impact on the rest of the system.

Systems can create amazing things, or they can become malignantly destructive. In my experience, these five rules of engagement drive the patterns of interaction that help create the former. This may take some time to instill in your team, but I have found that people very quickly warm to each idea. If you commit to reminding people regularly—weekly works well—then they take to it readily. These five rules also have the benefit of helping managers to align behavior in the short term. If the team is a system, then this enables you to make small adjustments to the patterns of interaction when they are at their most teachable moments. "Albert, will what you just said help make Jim want to be a job reference for you? No, I thought not. Now see if you can fix it right away."

A Practical Roadmap to Collaborative Decision Making

Once your team is starting to look like they are ready to design collaboratively, you'll need to guide them across our river of abductive reasoning. We know it probably won't take place in a straight line, but that doesn't mean it's just going to spontaneously happen; quite the opposite. If the design thinking process is not guided, you may well end on the wrong shore, get lost along the way, or simply land right where you started. The following process of collaborative decision-making will ensure an interdisciplinary approach to a difficult problem, engage the participants, and advance the solution to the next stage. More importantly, it will bring the participants closer as co-workers by fostering new connections and modeling collaborative behavior.

Businesspeople are generally trained to succeed and thrive in competitive environments, both inside and outside their organizations. This is a very good thing, except when it comes to situations where a team's inability to be collaborative leads to a weak solution to a challenge. Collaborative decision-making ("CDM") can be a powerful method to get to a solution when the problem itself is so messy that half the challenge is getting a handle on defining it before you even start. The following roadmap is a six-step process for facilitating CDM in groups of people who are experts in their subject matter but not necessarily in integrative collaboration techniques.

1. Gather the Right Group

A collaboration-based solution will only happen if the people involved have one part of the answer somewhere inside them. If the problem is complex, the team has to be diverse. And multidisciplinary. And interdisciplinary. Just like the Apollo 13 engineers needed to have all the bits and pieces available at their fingertips before they could synthesize the CO_2 scrubber, your team will also need to have the basic building blocks of a solution readily available. Don't worry about their ability to get along at this point. You will take care of that as part of the process. Whenever you get two or more people together, there will be politics and entrenched behavior patterns. You are going to help them to set that all aside as part of this process. First of all, make sure the raw materials for the solution are available to you. This does not always mean you need subject matter experts. Often those folks have a difficult time letting go of how they have been trained. That said, if you're creating a CO_2 scrubber, you'll need to have at least somebody on the team that knows about such things.

2. Role of Humility

As we mentioned previously, humility is a key part of the Focal Thinking process. Using CDM to tackle complex problems requires a level of humility because a collaborative, interdisciplinary, multi-dimensional approach to problem-solving requires the participants to be comfortable letting go of their idea the instant something better comes along. This is often the point where collaboration falls apart; when people's identity and personal value proposition is tied with always being The One With The Idea, or that person's cousin, The Smartest Person In The Room. A sense of good-natured humility is something that is often in short supply in most business contexts. Businesspeople are trained—formally at business school, and informally on the job—that humility is the one thing most likely to get you fired or worse: marginalized. In most business contexts, humility is tantamount to weakness, and in the rough-and-tumble world of survival of the fittest, humility will put you at the bottom of the food chain.

Here is the problem with that. When we get Darwinian and talk about survival of the fittest, we are misconstruing what Darwin meant. Even the most cursory reading of Darwin will show that he was referring to the species that best fit their environment (thus "fittest"); in other words, the one that best adapts to its surroundings. That species might not be the strongest, fastest, smartest, or have the biggest biceps, but it knows how to work with the others and what it finds in its immediate environment. Regardless of what you think of Darwin, the fact remains that for our society, survival of the fittest usually means survival of the bullheaded. We all have healthy egos, and that is well and good, but when you are facing an intractable, amorphous, difficult problem that demands the very best thinking from many different people with complementary perspectives, the bullheaded are doomed to extinction. And they're going to take everyone down with them.

3. Faking Humility

Although we need humility to collaborate effectively, that's not a quality that's easy to find, so sometimes you have to fake it. Understanding human nature and the reality that you can't magically instill the right amount of humility into hard-driving, power-hungry (i.e. "normal") people, how can CDM stand a chance? Easy! If the group does not have sufficient humility, get them to pretend they do. Assume that the team is made up of knowledgeable people with strong egos and the need to be right at all times. Here is how it can work.

Most of us don't actively listen to others, so that is the first place to start. We need to force them to actively listen to each other, without being seen to be forcing them. My favorite way to do this is a tactic used by improv actors, whose careers depend on their ability to not only listen to others but to build on what they have said immediately and creatively. Get your team in a circle around the room, have one person step forward and say three words, make a gesture, and step back. Then everybody in the circle—at the same time—steps forward and mimics precisely what that person said and did. If you do it right, it will look vaguely cultish and weird.

Please understand that I hate group exercises with a burning passion. There are those who love them, but that is not me. Despite my biases, the fact is that in the right setting, done the right way, they are incredibly powerful. This little exercise works for a few reasons. First, it forces people to listen to someone else actively. You have to pay attention, or you won't be able to mimic what they just did, and then you will look like a Non-Team Player. Second, it levels the playing field. I have done this exercise with pretty much any level of executives, professors, and employees. Nobody escapes the good-natured goofiness of this. If you are not able to break down the social hierarchy inherent in the group, or at least suspend it for a while, you will have a tough time instilling the kind of humility they will need to collaborate. Third, it lets people play a bit. Collaboration needs an element of fun, or it won't work, and this is a great way to start that mindset off. And I will promise you that there is always one person who does something downright goofy—usually the quietest one in the bunch. When this little exercise is done, you have started to get people to fake humility. They are now getting used to actively listening to each other, their status is temporarily suspended, and they are beginning to have a bit of fun.

4. The Analog

Now what? Wicked problems like we face in complex conflicts are "wicked" because they are amorphous and ill-defined, so if you are going to solve it, you need to pierce that veil of obscurity and drag it into the cold, hard light of reality. If you can't tackle the problem head-on, tackle the next closest thing that you can get your hands on. An effective way to do this is by creating an analog of the problem, work on solving that, and gradually work your way up to the real thing. An effective way to create the analog is to get them to embody the problem and start bringing it into reality somehow physically. The problem is amorphous, so force it into some physical form.

One way that works well is to get people into threes and challenge them to embody the interaction between a new brand and its customer. For example, two people are tasked with embodying a fictitious and unusual brand; the stranger the brand, the easier it will be to embody it. I like to use something like Apple Airlines because it is a brand most are familiar with, and it can be a useful thought experiment to imagine what that line extension might be like. The remaining person in the trio plays the role of the customer, and together, they all play out how the interaction between that brand and the customer might unfold. What is the counter staff like? How do the flight attendants behave? How is the cabin decorated? What do the other customers look like? What kind of food do they serve?

As people get comfortable creating this analog of the real problem, they can put aside their concerns of the day and get into the mindset of identifying elements of an experience that until a few minutes before did not even exist. By giving them the challenge of doing this with a problem that's only just out of their reach, you can warm them up for the main event to come, in which we'll start to add elements of the real problem at hand gradually. Now that the process is underway, it gets much more comfortable.

5. From Analog to Prototype

Once people have started engaging on the analog of the real problem and the juices are flowing, it is time to start the real work. At this stage, take the analog and turn it into a prototype of the actual solution you're looking for. Now it gets real. Here is an example. A recent client was a group of science educators who were challenged with the task of "increasing student engagement." This was a great example of an amorphous problem with no clear source or solution. I used the fictitious airline started by Apple and had them collaborating on what that brand experience might be like. When it came time to get down to the real problem at hand, I switched up the exercise like this: Now, instead of being airline representatives, they were school admissions professionals charged with the responsibility of explaining to parents how their school keeps students engaged. The effect on the room was electric. We had the right people in the room, they were primed and ready to collaborate, and they were warmed up and actively listening. Now that the real problem at hand was on the table, the room's energy went ballistic, as it always does at this stage.

The key to success at the prototype stage is to put people in a different frame of reference than they usually would be because looking at a challenge from another's perspective is an excellent way to make an old problem new again. In this case, it was professors playing the role of admissions and sales. In the process of selling something yet-to-be-created, they create the roadmap to the solution.

6. From Prototype to Solution

To this point, your people have engaged in small teams, and now it is time to get the entire group together. If you are going to be interdisciplinary, you need to make sure that all the different perspectives are mixed, and that may not have happened to this point. The process looks like this. Everyone needs to be together in as close a space as possible, comfortable, and practical. The moderator needs to have a large whiteboard (preferably two) available. Then you ask each small team to explain the outcome of their interaction. What was discussed? What was effective? What was persuasive? How did it feel? Then you encourage the groups to interact and discuss each other's experiences. This is where different perspectives start to emerge and engage with each other.

The role of the moderator at this stage is to act as a qualitative researcher, listening for emerging themes and noting them down on the whiteboard. By the end of this session, the whiteboard will be covered in thoughts, and the moderator will start circling common themes—preferably using a red-colored marker for clarity—and reflecting them to the team. The moderator should try to develop consensus from the group on the following items:

1. What do we agree on?
2. Where do we disagree?
3. What should we do next?
4. Who will lead the charge?

Once you have the right mindset in the team and you've got a semi-structured way for them to collaborate, the last step in the process is to make sure you've got your eyes open at all times to the constant change around you.

Agile Monitoring

The next element of resilience is agile monitoring and feedback. As we've been saying all along, in a dynamic conflict, it's not enough to have a strategy; you have to revisit the strategy continually. You don't need strategy meetings; you need revise-the-strategy-again sessions. You'll need to be monitoring the power base and the interaction shake-ups constantly so that they can pivot and change as new information comes in.

We know that a complex conflict is dynamic and will be in a constant state of change for as long as it exists. Our approach to making sense of it, therefore, needs not just to be able to tolerate change, but also to take advantage of it. Change should be a feature, not a bug. We want to show up to work in the morning excited to see what's changed since yesterday because we know that it's going to bring new opportunities for advancement. That's why I landed on the idea of using nonlinear dynamical systems theory as a way to make sense of complex conflicts in the first place. The unknown state of the outcome is not a reason to stand still. Quite the opposite: it demands constant attention.

As we do this, we need to be in a constant state of heightened awareness. With every step to the next stone, we need to make sure that we are making progress in the right direction. However, we also have to make some decisions about when we are going to take that calibration. Here is an example of what that means. I recently was able to lose a decent amount of weight. I treated myself like my own little science experiment and measured my calorie intake, so it stayed a level that would be less than my body expended. Not exactly groundbreaking science, but for me, it worked. My progress over the course of several months showed a consistent downward trend. However, it was not a straight line. There were times when I increased a bit instead of losing.

At those times, I had to re-evaluate my intake measurements and adjust. It is just as important when you measure as it is what you measure. At first, I weighed in every single day. Not only did that fail to give an accurate representation of the previous day's intake because of the lag time, but it also made me crazy. If you sample too often when you are dealing with a fluctuating measurement, that noise can distract you from what is going on. When I decided to weigh in once a week at the same time of day, the noise from micro-fluctuations went away, and I could evaluate my intake based on the entire week. I still had times when I was up in weight, but that enabled me to adjust for next week.

I suggest regular team updates to the human landscape model about every week as well. That will be regular enough to force everyone to revisit where everything stands with each of the participants, but not so often as to be overbearing or pointless. With most of my clients, I do a strategy update every week in which I review secondary content sources as well as primary research with folks on the ground. I pull out themes I see emerging or continuing on from when we originally created the model. In each theme, I make a point to cover the new facts that have emerged, what the power implications of those facts are, and suggest ideas for how to use that to shake up patterns of interaction. Those are then left up to the issues management teams to decide how they want to proceed.

Not everything that changes needs to be actioned. Not every new thing is a real opportunity. The process of creating that constant flow of updated information is important, but so is the ability to judge what should be actioned and what should not be. That's where it's crucial to triage the prioritization of incoming input effectively. The senior executives appreciate getting a big picture view of the situations, and the folks on the ground like to have that context to inform their specific objectives.

Find Your Own Bias

As I've said a few times, data don't become facts until someone decides that is what they are. That decision is based on judgment. At some point, you will take all the data you have gathered and see if it makes any sense. In an abductive, step-by-step sensemaking approach, there will never be a complete certainty. It is not possible despite all our wishful thinking, so don't try. That is how conflicts start in the first place, as we have discovered, because that way leads to the Coherence

Trap. At the stage where we have gathered facts and are re-evaluating progress, it is worth remembering what we are trying to accomplish in the first place. The point of our quest is to make sense of complex conflicts in a way that allows us to create strategy and adapt to the inevitable changes that occur along the way, so we can be called upon to know what to do next, and why. Using the Focal Thinking approach, we have a way to develop detailed strategies for accomplishing what we need to, and we have ways to pay attention to things as they change and adapt accordingly. But we're still missing one crucial last ingredient.

If you're paying attention to a complex conflict, chances are there's nothing neutral about your interest. Even if you don't care how the conflict unfolds, you still have an interest in the conflict itself. If you are digging into a conflict to the depth we are, you are definitely not neutral. So let's not pretend otherwise. When people claim neutrality, it usually means they are simply trying to validate their position by putting themselves in the mythical center. ("Why are all the news shows so right/left-wing these days?"). We have to be ruthlessly honest in our undertaking with Focal Thinking. Any other approach is doomed to failure because it will not be able to see everything that is going on.

Part of our analysis is knowing the lens through which we see the world, as well as that of others. If we are wearing rose-colored glasses, we need to realize that everything we are seeing takes on that hue. Because we are striving for reality, we need to adjust what we see for our own biases. When all we have is a hammer, everything starts looking like a nail. We need to accept that, acknowledge our own perspectives, and factor that into our own analysis.

Our experience of doing the analysis is just as valuable as the data themselves. For example, content analysis is a type of measurement methodology designed to pull meaning from existing information such as text, transcripts, video, etc. Modern content analysis experts have realized that because content is designed to be experienced, researchers will be more effective if they include their own experience of engaging with the content into their final analysis. We are not dispassionate automatons when it comes to making sense of content, and any pretense that we are neutral only serves to cloud the analysis. To be genuinely unbiased, we have to factor our non-neutrality out of the equation. That means acknowledging the biases and perceptions through which we filter the information we are making sense of.

The final step in the sensemaking approach, then, is to openly acknowledge our biases and observe ourselves as we observe the data. This is a meta-analysis: an observation about the very act of observing. Here is an example. Among other things, I am a communications professional, and I know that I tend to view all problems as communications failures. I know that I gravitate towards sensemaking explanations that include a communications component.

Not only is that comfortable for me because of my training, but I also happen to think that it does help explain the data I observe. Focal Thinking is a good example. It is based on the work of many others, all of which happens to point to the fact that conflicts are driven by inadequate communication. Did I gravitate there because when I discovered that it fit my world view? Absolutely. Does that mean Focal Thinking is wrong? Of course not. If it works, it works. What it does mean, however, is that when I came across the foundational elements of Focal Thinking, I needed to realize that I might have been experiencing confirmation bias. That meant I needed to redouble my efforts to ensure I was not just reinforcing my own preferences. Given that this approach is supported by the work of a wide range of disciplines, including social psychologists and engineers, I felt comfortable with the fact that it was not just my biases showing through.

Before you can make sense of complexity, you need to acknowledge your own biases. This is a difficult thing to do because we experience the world as individuals, and we are each the center of our own universe. We are centrists, and the rest of the world is left-wing. Or right-wing. We are safe drivers, and everyone else drives like maniacs. We are intelligent, and everyone else is just a bit dumber than we are. We are sane, and others are just a bit crazy. It's human nature. So what are your biases? It would help if you got that out on the table right now. Here are some ways to do that.

Pretend you are introducing yourself to a potential romantic interest. Someone you trust implicitly, whom you want to have a deep understanding of your mind and emotions. In an unguarded moment, how would you explain to that person who you truly are? "Truth be told, I am actually kind of _____." Imagine what you would tell that person if you wanted them to know you. You can also look back at your professional history. If you have been in communications forever, chances are you look at the world through that lens. If you are an engineer, chances are you look at the world quantitatively, and if something cannot fit on a spreadsheet, you might not give it full credence. Your background is a good place to start when finding your own biases. Not only does that tell you how you have been trained to think, but it also can be an indicator of where you are most comfortable since you have gravitated there over the years.

The Resilience Cycle

It may be helpful to think of resilience as a cycle with three stages: Observe, analyze, and adjust. In the context of complex conflicts, here's what that might look like for you.

Observe: Once we have the prototype solution in place, we can take that first step to that first stone in the river. However, before we dip our foot into the rushing waters, we need to figure out how we will know if there is a stone there. This will depend on the circumstances. If the river is clear, we will be able to see the stone under the surface. If the water is deep or opaque, we will need to decide how we will tell where the next stone is. Will we use our toe to poke around until it hits something? Will we grab a long stick at probe for a hard spot? Will we jump in the direction of where we hope the stone is? Just because we are taking a leap of faith into the unknown does not mean we cannot also be scientific about it. Or at least methodical.

As we mentioned earlier, you'll want to focus on tracking the actions and interactions of the other participants in the conflict. This is more like intelligence-gathering than perception research. You want to track actions. Who is meeting with whom? Who said what on social media? Who is running a communications campaign? How are people talking about the conflict? This sort of behavior will give you insight into the kind of impact you need to have or are already having.

Analyze: Once you have some observations on patterns of interaction, you will need to connect that all back to your conflict map. Going back to our Northern Gateway example, if we wanted to soften up the federal government's vocal stance against the project by finding ways to align the environmental/producer/province coalition, we would want to map the actions of key players back to that strategy. If we found, for example, that a federal minister had expressed interest in participating in a GHG emission reduction conference and we know the coalition players would be there, we would want to factor that into our persuasion plan. How might we provide the minister with value as part of that conference so that we could, at some point, ask her for consideration of our position?

As data come in regarding the actions and interactions of key participants in the Conflict Driver and Influencer groups, you will need to continually keep your conflict map updated so that you can adjust as that new information comes in. I would suggest, however, that the volume of data is less critical than the frequency of its collection in the context of complex conflicts. We can quibble about how granular and detailed the information should be, but there is no doubt that stale information is not valuable. If, for example, you focus your effort on following every meeting that the relevant government official has, and yet you lose sight of the fact that another participant has completely changed their approach and signaled as such on their social media feed, you will have done yourself a disservice. As you allocate finite data collection resources to balance your data-collecting efforts, you may need to prioritize that which is timely over that which is detailed.

Adjust

One of the most critical impediments to adjusting to new information is the sunk cost effect. One key to being resilient is the ability to overcome the sunk cost effect, which happens when you stick with the current course of action primarily because you have already put so much effort and resources into it. We all want to be consistent and committed. Our coworkers expect it, our shareholders demand it, and we have been taught to value it. This only becomes a problem, however, when not supported by the facts. If a current course of action is not working, staying with it can quickly turn from commitment into stubbornness. The trick is to know the difference.

In many cases, however, the trick is to know there even is a trick to begin with. Many people are not self-aware enough to know that they may be acting from the sunk cost effect, and awareness, as they say, is the first step. We know innovation requires a step-by-step prototyping process that nimbly identifies and adjusts to incoming data. Where the sunk cost effect carries sway, it is virtually impossible for people to say to themselves or their peers, "That wasn't quite right, so let's try something a bit different." This is not a failure of human pride, vanity or ego. It's a failure of leadership. When leaders signal to their organizations that failure will not be tolerated, they're saying that they are incapable of organizationally adapting to signals from their environment. As we discussed earlier, we need to prioritize resilience over consistency in the case of complex conflicts.

Innovation is not always the appropriate strategy. But when it is, leadership must signal that the organization expects that people will repeatedly fail and on an accelerated timeline. In other words, "Let's fail faster and more often, and do it before we put out anything we can't take back." This demands a corporate culture that is the polar opposite of the sunk cost effect.

Wrap-Up and What's Next

This chapter will have given you some practical tools to stay resilient in the face of the inevitable changes that come with complex conflict: creating the right team dynamic, getting them primed for doing design thinking, making collaborative decisions together, monitoring the situation as it unfolds with a clear-eyed awareness of your own biases, and managing the resilience cycle. For many of my clients, the issues management teams that follow these principals are very sought-after postings. Despite the stress and pressure, this type of working environment can be very rewarding. The advertising guru David Ogilvy was said to be of the opinion that if people aren't having fun, they're not going to be creative. I'm not sure if navigating complex conflicts counts as fun, but there's merit to the idea that it should at least be rewarding.

Next, we'll wrap things up and provide you with some ways to keep in touch with me and other like-minded Focal Thinkers.

Let's Stay Connected

Now you have a pretty detailed roadmap that will help you overcome the Coherence Trap, get to a state of Heathrow-esque ROR, and ultimately equip you with the ability to show strategic leadership in the face of complex conflicts. If you follow the Focal Thinking approach, you're going to be able to tell people what to do next and why to do it. That's going to put you in a solid position regardless of whether you're a leader, an advisor, or a participant in a complex conflict.

As I mentioned at the beginning, I genuinely want you to win. I want this because if you win, then the world is going to be a better place. I care less about your projects and more about how you're going to make a difference by reinvigorating all those dried-up patterns of interaction and creating new bases for engagement and connection.

Thank you for spending this time with me. I'd love to stay in touch and for you to connect with other Focal Thinkers. I've developed several online platforms for us to stay connected, so we can all help each other out as we put these principles, plans, and concepts to use.

Here's where we can find each other:

- focalthinking.com/FightDifferent
- Twitter: @FightDifferent
- Instagram: @Fight_Different
- LinkedIn: "Fight Different" Group

Talk soon!

Acknowledgments

The author would like to thank all the amazing people who made this book possible. My doctoral committee, Dr. Tom Keenan, Dr. Marco Musiani, Dr. Loren Falkenberg, Dr. Mehdi Mourali, and Dr. Kevin Seel. Dr. Jim Dewald, who got my academic career started and has never stopped encouraging me. Dr. Kunal Basu, who showed me how to combine arts, authorship and academia. Bryce Tingle and Hugh McFadyen, the wiser two-thirds of the Trilateral Ecumenical Commission. My clients, who pushed me to turn an interesting academic diversion into a practical approach to bringing about real change. Chris Bedford, who gave me the freedom and the vision to pursue my research. Dr. Roger Martin, whose presentation on Design Thinking changed the course of my life. My friends and business partners, David Pfeiffer and Sheenah Rogers-Pfeiffer, who understood this all from the beginning. My sister, Dr. Michelle Suderman, who lead the way and paved a path so well that even I could follow it. My cousin, Dr. Terry Linhart, who taught me the value of getting up before dawn to "do the paper route." The Adams and Lee families—the best "steps" I could ever hope for. And most of all, my (very) longsuffering wife, Viv, and kids, Michael and Jennifer, whose patience has shown no end.

About the Author

 When a challenge is complex, the solution needs to be diverse. Dr. Mark Szabo, BA, MBA, JD, PhD brings that much-needed diverse perspective to complex conflicts. His background in consulting, communications, law and academia enables him to draw on the aspects of multiple disciplines that are needed to tackle complex conflicts and situations. To keep balance in the midst of it all, Dr. Szabo plays bass guitar, walks obsessively, thrives on time with his wife and kids, and enjoys seeing those kids grow into the kind of adults he aspires to be someday.

References and Further Reading

[1] Holiday, R. (2019). *Stillness is the Key*. New York: Portfolio/Penguin. pp. 75-79.

[2] Coleman, P. T., Vallacher, R. R., Nowak, A., & Bui-Wrzosinska, L. (2007). Intractable conflict as an attractor: A dynamical systems approach to conflict escalation and intractability. *American Behavioral Scientist, 50*(11), 1454–1476.

[3] Vallacher, R. R., Coleman, P. T., Nowak, A., & Bui-Wrzosinska, L. (2010). Rethinking intractable conflict: The perspective of dynamical systems. *The American Psychologist, 65*(4), 262–278.

[4] Coleman, P. T., Nowak, A., Bui-Wrzosinska, L., Bartoli, A., Liebovitch, L. S., Musallam, N., & Kugler, K. G. (2011). *The Five Percent: Finding Solutions to Seemingly Impossible Conflicts* (1st ed.). New York City: PublicAffairs.

[5] Vallacher, R. R., Coleman, P. T., Nowak, A., & Bui-Wrzosinska, L. (2010). Rethinking intractable conflict: The perspective of dynamical systems. *The American Psychologist, 65*(4), 262–278.

[6] Vallacher, R. R., Coleman, P. T., Nowak, A., Bui-Wrzosinska, L., Liebovitch, L., Kugler, K., & Bartoli, A. (2013). *Attracted to conflict: Dynamic roundations of destructive social relations*. Heidelberg: Springer. p. 3.

[7] Andrade, L., Plowman, D. A., & Duchon, D. (2008). Getting Past Conflict Resolution: A Complexity View of Conflict. *Emergence: Complexity & Organization, 10*(1), 23–38.

[8] Deutsch, M. (1973). *The Resolution of Conflict: Constructive and Destructive Processes*. New Haven, CT: Yale University Press.

[9] Vallacher, et al. (2013), ibid., p. 20.

[10] Coleman, et al. (2007), ibid., p. 1455.

[11] Vallacher, et al. (2010), ibid., p. 263.

[12] Merçay, A., & Borrie, J. (2006). A physics of diplomacy? The dynamics of complex social phenomena and their implications for multilateral negotiations. In J. Borrie & V. M. Randin (Eds.), *Thinking Outside the Box in Multilateral Disarmament and Arms Control Negotiations*. Geneva: United Nations. p. 151.

[13] Smith, E. R., & Conrey, F. R. (2007). Agent-based modeling: a new approach for theory building in social psychology. *Personality and Social Psychology Review: An Official Journal of the Society for Personality and Social Psychology, Inc, 11*(1), p. 87.

[14] Campbell, M. C. (2003). Intractability in environmental disputes: Exploring a complex construct. *Journal of Planning Literature, 17*(3), p. 362.

[15] Vallacher et al. (2010), ibid., p. 262.

[16] Bush, R. A. B., & Folger, J. P. (1994). *The Promise of Mediation: Responding to Conflict Through Empowerment and Recognition*. San Francisco: Jossey-Bass.

[17] Davis, C. B., & Lewicki, R. J. (2003). Environmental conflict resolution: Framing and intractability. *Environmental Practice, 5*(3), p. 200.

[18] Davis, C. B., & Lewicki, R. J. (2003), ibid.

[19] Shefrin, H. & Statman, M. (2003). The Contributions of Daniel Kahneman and Amos Tversky. *The Journal of Behavioral Finance, 4*(2), 54–58

[20] Kilgour, D. M., & Hipel, K. W. (2005). The graph model for conflict resolution:

Past, present, and future. *Group Decision and Negotiation, 14*(6), 441–460.

[21] Kolko, J. (2010). Abductive thinking and sensemaking: The drivers of design synthesis, *Design Issues*, 26(1), p. 20.

[22] Lockwood, T. (2009). Transition: How to Become a More Design-Minded Organization. *Design Management Review, 20*(3), 28–37.

Martin, R. (2009). *The Design of Business.* Boston: Harvard Business School Publishing.

Verganti, R. (2009). *Design-Driven Innovation.* Boston: Harvard Business School Publishing.

[23] Merçay, A., & Borrie, J. (2006), ibid., p. 152.

[24] Nelson, H. & Stolterman, E., (2014), *The Design Way.* Boston: MIT Press.

[25] Brooks, G. (2015). *Unfinished Business, Jorn Utzon returns to the Sydney Opera House.* New Yorker Magazine, October 10, 2015.

[26] Krippendorff, K. (2006). *The Semantic Turn: A New Foundation for Design.* Boca Raton: Taylor & Francis Group, LLC.

[27] Johnson, S. (2010), *Where Good Ideas Come From: The Natural History of Innovation*, New York: Riverhead Books.

[28] Rittel, H. W. J., & Webber, M. M. (1973). Dilemmas in a general theory of planning. *Policy Sciences, 4*, 155–169.

[29] Asah, S. T., Bengston, D. N., Wendt, K., & Nelson, K. C. (2012). Diagnostic reframing of intractable environmental problems: Case of a contested multiparty public land-use conflict. *Journal of Environmental Management, 108*, 108–119.

[30] Gabbay, D., & Woods, J. (2006). Advice on abductive logic. *Logic Journal of IGPL, 14*(2), 189–219.

[31] Holiday, R. (2019), ibid., p.14.

[32] Ivison, J. (2014). In Canada, even a pipeline project supported by the NDP is not sure thing. *National Post.* November 21, 2014.

[33] Lantin, P., & Vernonis, C. (2015). Opinion: Northern Gateway opposition building steam. *Edmonton Journal.* July 2, 2015.

[34] Hussain, Y. (2015). Oil-by-rail economics suffers amid narrowing spreads, *Financial Post.* February 9, 2015.

Mayeda, A., (2014), Ottawa readies aboriginal treaty push amid pipeline opposition. *Financial Post.* September 26, 2014.

[35] Coleman, et al. (2011), ibid.

[36] Fisher, R., & Ury, W., (1991), *Getting to Yes: Negotiating an Agreement Without Giving In.* New York: Random House Business Books.

[37] Coleman, et al. (2011), ibid., p.124-133.

[38] Kotter, John P., (1996), *Leading Change.* Boston: Harvard Business School Press.

Made in the USA
Columbia, SC
20 November 2020